ROGUE

An exploration of human domestication

PRIMATE

JOHN A. LIVINGSTON

KEY PORTER BOOKS

Canadian Cataloguing in Publication Data

Livingston, John A.
Rogue Primate

Includes bibliographical references and index.
ISBN: 1-55013-508-2

1. Ecology — Philosophy. 2. Human ecology. 3. Man — Influence on nature. 4. Technology — Moral and ethical aspects. I. Title.

QH540.5.L58 1993   304.2   C93-094120-9

Key Porter Books Limited
70 The Esplanade
Toronto, Ontario
Canada M5E 1R2

The publisher acknowledges the assistance of the
Canada Council and the Ontario Arts Council.

Design: Annabelle Stanley
Printed and bound in Canada

94 95 96 97 98 99 6 5 4 3 2 1

CONTENTS

PREFACE

It took me a good many years to fully accept that the necessary (not merely the proper) study of humankind is itself. Having spent the greater part of a lifetime absorbed in the appreciation and the attempted understanding of living phenomena that are not human, while at the same time ceaselessly advocating their protection, preservation, and "conservation," it was not easy to pause and evaluate the effectiveness — and logic — of that advocacy. But for my own peace of mind it needed doing. So in 1977 I did a critical analysis and wrote it up, then looked at what I had wrought for almost four years before publishing it. It was going to cost me, and it did.

At the time of its publication, the American environmental teacher and essayist Joseph Meeker observed that my *Fallacy of Wildlife Conservation* appeared to be a book written in blood. It was indeed painful to have to acknowledge that the fundamental premises of the conventional conservation argument to which I had long adhered were radically flawed. It was even more painful to discover that rather than alleviating the parlous circumstances of the non-human world, the conventional conservation argument actually makes those circumstances worse. In that book I characterized customary wildlife conservation advocacy as a "catechism" that I for one had been uncritically mouthing for too long.

In a nutshell, the fallacy is the generally unchallenged belief that wild, undomesticated plants and animals and their communities can be enabled to survive the human presence on Earth by means of their careful safekeeping within the rational, managerial framework of "resource conservation." The belief is fallacious because to see any phenomenon as a "resource" is to see it as a human utility or amenity. Such a perception precludes the possibility of any non-quantifiable worth residing in that phenomenon — even to itself. Its value becomes purely instrumental. If such value cannot be shown, and in practice even if it can, the non-human is permitted to continue to exist solely at the human pleasure. Since resource conservation does not allow worth (to itself) to inhere in Nature, it can protect Nature only as the human estate, in which case it is no longer Nature but rather an extension of the human apparatus. However argued or presented, resource conservation is a wholly proprietary, human-chauvinist concept.

Here I mean resource conservation not as a practice or a policy, but as an *idea*. As such it requires the prior perception of the non-human world, and our relationship with it, in a very particular way. For any living being to be able to see other living beings as commodities or utilities would strike any naturalist as anomalous, even bizarre. Could it be possible for any non-human entity to see the world as its exclusive property, its vested estate, its heritage, its right and privilege, its fief? Surely not. But — especially in its Western, Euro-American form (or perhaps we should say its northern, industrial form) — the human animal does just that.

Something is askew here. It follows that the study of the human animal becomes unavoidable. As it turned out, I was not as lonely in that view as I had thought. Some years earlier I had learned of the existence of a number of like minds through the response to *One Cosmic Instant: A Natural History of Human Arrogance*, in which I first tried to show the human destruction of Nature as a cultural and ideological phenomenon.

Those books and sundry articles in a similar vein put me in touch with many people who had been thinking about various aspects of the cultural dimension of the human conquest of Nature. In more recent years there has been a quite spectacular burgeoning of critical and creative thought on questions of the relationship between human belief systems, human ideas, and the destruction of Nature. Indeed, such endeavours have far transcended the relatively limited field of wildlife preservation, addressing virtually all aspects of modern culture.

This work goes by a variety of names, including ecosophy, environmental thought, environmental philosophy, environmental ethics, and ecophilosophy.[1] The term "deep ecology" is used by some. All of it may loosely be described as social and cultural criticism from an "ecologic" bias. (Studies in these fields do not necessarily flow from the science of ecology, but do proceed from the basic principle of total interrelatedness that ecology suggests.) Contributions to this body of thought come from both the sciences and the humanities, and although there are many interpretations, perhaps the most pervasive in the ecophilosophical community at the present time is that the "antidote" to our modern ways of dealing with the world is not technological, not scientific, not even ethical. The modern challenge is metaphysical and ontological — indeed, cosmological.

Now this may or may not be an accurate diagnosis, but if it is even partially correct, then the modern challenge is to our received ways of perceiving and apprehending the nature of reality and the nature of being in the universe. I am not going to pursue that further here; a rich and nutritious feast of elegant and persuasive thought on that subject has been laid before us in the last few years.[2] But I shall use it to make a point.

When I say that the present lamentable condition of non-human Nature is chargeable to our received wisdom, I am identifying the need for some change or correction in our ways of internalizing or ingesting the world around us. Take, for example, the problem of the worldwide diminishment of plant and animal populations, species, and whole biotas. A resource administrator would probably say that the problem is one of inadequate or ineffectual management, which could be corrected by beefed-up development strategies. A computer expert would likely blame our theoretical models, and recommend enhanced predictive capability. A wildlife biologist would cite the sparseness of our fundamental knowledge of the biology of threatened species.

There are still others who define the problem of diminishing species and habitats as a consequence of the gulf between the have and the have-not nations, the ultimate solution resting in a committed movement toward international human parity through economic development and strategic resource utilization. There are those who insist that non-human species are being pushed and elbowed from the planet by the sheer weight and pressure of human numbers. Others say that we must devise, promulgate, and recognize "rights" for non-human phenomena toward the "liberation" of Nature from human tyranny. And then there are those who feel that the mischief resides, at root, in the world-views and belief systems that allow people to see non-human Nature in the despotic, utilitarian, objectively distanced, and alienated ways we do.

Each of these approaches suggests its preferred solution. Over and above the usual technical fixes, there have been many calls for an "environmental ethic." There are just as many calls for a new metaphysics. These often take the form of typologies or taxonomies of "paradigms" — the destructive, inappropriate, un-ecological, primitively dualistic, and mechanistic version which presently prevails, against which is opposed and contrasted an ideal interpretation for the New Age of human-ecosphere harmony. (Many of the latter are unabashedly humanistic, economistic, and resourcistic.)[3]

I will not need to stress that no one knows how a new paradigm or a new metaphysic, no matter how cogently drafted, is to be gotten into the human bloodstream. You don't legislate things of this kind. You evolve into them, and out of them. That takes time. The current version goes back at least to the Renaissance. Some place its origins in classical antiquity. Some see it arising as early as the dawn of sedentism and agriculture. I believe it emerged earlier, and will argue my case in due course.

All of these definitions are perfectly legitimate, and all of them, in their way, are correct. That is, they are correct so long as we agree that the implied remedies are correct also. That becomes a matter of opinion. We all have our preferred solutions, which means that we all have our preferred problem definitions. Most often, those definitions will fall between or combine or otherwise incorporate more than one of the examples I have used. But I think it would be accurate to say that relatively few positions on problem definition/solution go so far as to isolate the human *being* as the focus. Not so much what we do, or even what we think, but what we *are*. The human animal as an evolved biological phenomenon. The animal with something askew.[4]

ACKNOWLEDGMENTS

I thank Graeme Gibson and M.T. Kelly for having discerned publishability in this work, and for having taken steps toward that end.

I thank Jonathan Webb of Key Porter for many sensitive and skilful editorial contributions.

I thank the configuration of the planets one sunny day many years ago, when, over bag lunch on a campus lawn, my late dear friend and colleague John E. Page conspired with me to begin the study of cultural and historical perspectives of Nature.

I thank Neil Evernden, scholar, co-worker, and friend, for the years of insight and inspiration he has so unselfishly afforded me, both by his example and by his intellectual and personal generosity.

I thank a long succession of gifted and relentless graduate students in the Faculty of Environmental Studies at York University for never letting me off the hook. They are far too many to list, but for special reasons I record my indebtedness to dian marino and Leesa Fawcett.

I thank Blitz, Una, Komakuk, Christie, Little Bear, and Big Max for allowing me to learn from them about interspecies self-identity.

For Ursula

THE
PROBLEM
ANIMAL

What human beings have visited upon this planet may legitimately be seen as an ecospheric holocaust. Only four times before, to the best of contemporary knowledge, have there been mass extinction events as dramatic as that which is unfolding today. They occurred 65, 94, 213, and 248 million years ago.[1] Those, of course, were "natural." To the extent that we are witnessing the effect of the proliferation of a single species, then the denudation of the planet could also be seen, dispassionately, as a natural biological circumstance.

On the other hand, if human *ideas* propel the flaming juggernaut, then perhaps ideas are amenable to change, and the process may be alleviated or stalled altogether. After all, ideas are not carried in our genes. They are carried in our heads, and they are subject to shuffling, revision, and adaptive modification. Like breeding stock in domesticated plants and animals, ideas may be selected

1

artificially and deliberately. This does not mean, however, that it is not natural to have ideas, or that the human species is not naturally the ideological species. What it does suggest is that some mix of biological and cultural ingredients is at work here.

This is not another essay into the nature/nurture controversy. It is enough to say that the human species would seem to be one in which nurture plays a relatively greater role than it does in some others. Species of our sort (and there are quite a few of them) are predisposed by nature ("preadapted") to receive and retain that nurturing. Nurturing, whether in a cave or a classroom, is culturing. And although we like to think that we teach our children, the active ingredient in the culturing process is their *learning*.

Learning of some kind is no doubt important for all species, certainly for birds and mammals, but it is especially important for those who are highly social — those who live in cohesively knit societies. Learning is even more important for those animals who live in socially *cooperative* societies. It is one thing to belong to a loose aggregation of hoofed grazers or browsers, in which individuals largely fend for themselves. It is quite another thing to belong to a society such as that of lions, in which individual members, according to age and sex, have particular roles or functions to perform, in defence, in hunting, in child care, or in some other way. Young lions have much to learn, and it takes them a long time to learn it; their successful nurturing is essential to the continuity of their society.

When they are little, lion cubs begin to learn by observation. When they are large enough, they learn by paws-on practice. Most retain the benefits of these experiences sufficiently well to be able to help take care of themselves and their families when the time comes. Probably the bulk of lion learning is experiential, not abstract. This is not to say that abstraction is unknown in the mind of a lion; on the basis of hunting methods, which include strategic deployment and ambushes, it is clear that there is more going on than simple reflexes. But it is probably safe to say that lions are not bogged down from day to day in abstract indecision about what should be done next, or why. They learn what they *need* to learn, they do what they *need* to do. They are not perfect at it; all predators are unsuccessful part of the time, because predation is a grindingly hard way to make a living.[2] But they are good enough, and that is what matters.

Young lions must however learn a great deal more than killing skills. They must learn what food is fit to eat, where it is, how it moves, when it moves, what is safe to tackle, what is the most easily obtained. (A predator usually takes the line of least resistance; even a relatively minor injury could seriously impair its ability to hunt successfully.) Once the food is obtained, and members of the family assemble around it, there comes into play a subtle and intricate ritual governing the feast itself. This too must be learned.

And there is much more to lion nurture than even this. There are the maintenance of social cohesiveness, the development of the sense of social and physical place, individual and group identity, and more. Lions do not carry this knowledge, or these skills, in their genes. The ineptness and "infantility," even in adulthood, of the lioness Elsa of the famous book and movie *Born Free* showed dramatically that a lion without lion nurture is not a lion any more. The animals we see in zoos are not lions; they are zoo lions. Lions are preadapted to receive and act upon lion nurture, not human nurture.

The individual lion, in the wild, learns to receive and apprehend the world in certain ways. We cannot know what the universe of a lion looks or feels like, but perhaps we can achieve an inkling by contrasting the graceless, apathetic, almost catatonic look of an overfed captive zoo-bred lion with the appearance of a real lion. Ninety percent of all the lions that I have ever seen in the wild were asleep. They sleep most of the time — or at least doze. But during that hour or two around dusk of the usual day when they must go to work, they are transformed.

The overwhelming impression conveyed by a hunting lioness (this task is performed mostly by females) is *total awareness*. As she walks, we cannot so much as guess at the variety and nature of the information she is synthesizing simultaneously, instantaneously. Then, when her attention zeros in on her selected target, her face and body convey an intensity of concentration so powerful that its energy emanation is almost palpable. This effect is not produced by mere hunger, nor, I think, only by the clear intentionality of the moment, but rather by absolute involvement — the focusing of her entire universe in this single act, here and now. All of her sensory apparatus is cued to the instant, and all the potential explosiveness of muscle and sinew is gathered and controlled by a hair-trigger. But there is more to it than even that. The hunting lioness in that moment is the evolutionary miracle personified. She is at once manifestation and process, means and end. She is all of life, all of time. She is utter, and consummate.

Then she moves. The planets begin to revolve again, and we are back to the real world of daily provisioning. But that single, ineffable fragment of eternity is graven into my sensibility forever. What happens next is incidental. The kill itself is usually sloppy by our standards, especially if there are inexperienced lions involved. But it gets done, and from all points of the compass members of the family in the neighbourhood begin trudging toward dinner. A nearby jackal has heard the commotion, and a white-backed vulture doing its last circle of the departing day has seen it. A band of hyenas takes note. The word gets around in a hurry. All interested parties in the community file the news, and those who are not interested go about their usual business.

4

I referred to biological memory. This is not to suggest that one has ever been a lion, or that one has ever been eaten by a lion. But somewhere, deep and far beyond the shifting clouds of memory, sometime, one was *wild*. The experience of the lioness was the fleeting, elusive, bittersweet re-cognition of wildness. Not a recollection of the mind, but a tingling, prickling, participatory kindling of the flesh. For a precious instant I have rejoined. For one moment of arrested infinity, my human alienation dissolves. I am home, and when I feel it I recognize it instantly. I recognize also, with terrible sadness, that I had forgotten to miss it.

Wildness receives a good deal of pejorative treatment in our society. It connotes desolation (usually meaning the absence of people), as well as barbarous savagery and all else that goes with the "primitive" condition, perhaps especially chaotic unpredictability and uncontrollability, both of which are anathema to all of the organizing principles of our technoculture. To be wild is to be ungovernable, which means uncivilized.

On the other hand, in spite of this culturally conditioned reflex to the quality of wildness, there remains in us a paradoxical fascination with that quality. As it is with so many contemporary social phenomena, we need look no farther than the world of commerce, especially advertising, for evidence of that fascination. At its extreme, it may be seen in some of the more outlandish high fashion advertisements, especially those having to do with the skins of dead predatory beings. The wildness of the dead carnivore is transferred to the human model, conferring upon her the mystery and excitement of the untamed. A less dramatic but more pervasive image of wildness is purveyed by every run-of-the-mill rock band, with what has become an ultraconventional re-enactment of stereotypical uncivilized behaviour. Another is in the growing popularity of "adventure" tourism to "exotic" (usually meaning wild or at least semi-natural) destinations.

If modern commerce sees exploitability in wildness, we may be sure that there is something in it. But is the advertiser playing upon some deep-seated, primal *need* in us, or merely helping, or indeed manipulating, us to the point at which a crass "want" becomes in our mind a gnawing need? An interesting literature has developed around this question,[3] but for present purposes the question is less the manipulation, more the apparent presence in us of the capacity, or even the need, to be manipulated. This would suggest the very opposite of wildness — passive dependence on some external agency of direction and control.

Even granting that possibility, however, at the same time there would seem to be within us some rarely expressed but still latent predisposition for wildness. I believe there is, but I also believe that it has become little more than vestigial, as the result of hundreds of thousands of years of both biological and cultural evolution. I could not "hold onto" my experience with the lioness. It was there, and then it was gone. I did my best to retain it, but my humanness prevailed.

But the cultural preoccupation with wildness remains. The qualities of emancipated ungovernability, unpredictability, and uncontrollability are of basic importance here, evoking as they do feelings both of resentment and of fear. Such feelings are often masked by contempt (wildness is "beneath" us), but that is no more than intellectual legerdemain. The resentment and fear are real, and both of them have ancient and legitimate roots. They have been magnified, intensified, and reinforced in our cultural tradition over a few thousand years, but I suspect that their origins long antedate our written (and perhaps even our oral) traditions.

Characteristically enough, there is in us a totally opposite apprehension of wildness. It finds its civilized expression in Nature appreciation in many forms, perhaps especially in the wilderness preservation movement and allied activities, both individual and collective. Although the source and locus of our Nature appreciation is often blurred by social overlays (literature, custom, institutions, ideas), it probably springs at least as much from the biological part of our being as from any other. Presumably the overwhelming attraction of Nature is that it is alive and wild, and at least for some, its attraction is enhanced by the fact that it is not of human manufacture.

(In the interest of ease and simplicity, I have chosen for purposes of this essay to speak of Nature when I am referring to those life phenomena that are not human, and to use more particular language when I am referring to the "generic" life totality of which we are part. No taint of misanthropy should be attached to this. Nor should my usage be construed as an exercise in the "personification" of our non-human surround. I am aware of these and other pitfalls in opting for convenience.)

Our responses to Nature are not only inherent in us, but are also products of our socialization and other learning experiences. Of all the possible examples of human askewness, our ambivalence about Nature and our own place in the natural world is as revealing as any other. We fear and are fascinated, celebrate and desecrate, commune and consume, deify and defile. We are of biological process, yet not of Nature. We exalt and even worship Nature, yet in such diverse activities as medicine and aerospace we seek relentlessly and fanatically to escape the surly bonds of our own nature. These kinds of mixed feelings about both Nature and the quality of wildness are deeply embedded in human cultures, and perhaps especially in our own.

It is a commonplace belief that the human animal is "the" cultural animal. This is simply not accurate. Any society, human or otherwise, in which modes of behaviour (techniques, rituals, language, etc.) are modified over time and are learned by members of that society in their modified form is cultural. The emergence of new dialects in honeybees or herring gulls is a cultural phenomenon; the use of tools for foraging by chimpanzees or Galapagos finches, the use of stones for breaking ostrich eggs by Egyptian vultures, ritual food-washing by Japanese macaques, and tree climbing by the lions of Lake Manyara are all cultural events.

All cultures are series of events, frozen for our analytic convenience at any given moment. My colleague John Page used to emphasize to his students that to use the word "culture" as a mere noun, and thus to imply an end or static state, is not particularly helpful. The richer, dynamic usage of the word is as a verb: culturing as an activity. Cultures are never fixed, never locked in. They are ceaselessly changing, mutating, shifting to accommodate new circumstances. Cultures are plastic, adaptive, temporary emergences, even more ephemeral than the species who create them.

Most non-human culturing activity appears to be of secondary importance in the daily exercise of being. It consists chiefly of adjustments or refinements — a local modification of language, an alternative method of foraging, a shift in social manners to fit a new situation, a little extra measure of convenience. But by and large these learned behavioural adjustments are modest; they change little in a species' functioning in its community. No matter the dialect, a honeybee is still a pollinator and a gull is still an all-purpose scavenger–predator. A climbing lion is still a top carnivore. Culturing in Nature is kept in proportion, as it were; it would not be seemly, nor perhaps good for its community or itself, were a species to become *too* engaged in novelty. And certainly not for novelty's own sake.

Alfred Romer, the great vertebrate palaeontologist, used to call attention to the inherent *conservatism* of evolutionary innovation. "Romer's Rule," as it has become, holds that "the initial survival value of a favourable innovation is conservative, in that it renders possible the maintenance of a traditional way of life in the face of changed circumstances."[4] Romer used to illustrate his point by reference to the ancient crossopterygian or lobe-finned fishes which were the first vertebrates to venture onto the land, and the progenitors of all terrestrial vertebrates. The earliest of these, stranded on some mud flat, struggled back to the water with the aid of rudimentary lungs and sturdy fins. In the usual conservative fashion, they were able thus — at least for a time — to go on being fishes. That some of them radically changed and eventually evolved into full-time air-breathing terrestrial animals was incidental.[5]

Whether Romer's Rule explains the apparent conservatism of most non-human cultural innovation I cannot say. In spite of picking up the habit of washing its potatoes, a Japanese macaque is still just that, and whether its novel feeding method could ever become an evolutionary determinant is impossible to know.

Other things being equal, culturing in Nature may or may not have evolutionary significance. If the products of culturing assist individual beings to continue to go about their "old ways" under changed conditions, then perhaps they may have historic importance. If, on the other hand, like some modest physical mutations that may arise, they are *not disadvantageous*, then perhaps their continued presence does not matter one way or another. In any case, it would appear that in non-human Nature the culturing process, though clearly visible in so many species, seems to be no more than one of an infinite inventory of powers, potentialities, and possibilities inherent in animals who are not human. It may be important to a group, or to a population, or even to a whole species, but it may not to most others.

For the human species, however, culturing has become overwhelmingly important. For many years, sundry biologists and humanists (I am aware that the distinction is largely artificial) have maintained that human biological evolution is over, and that we have attained a level of "development" qualitatively different from and "higher" than that of any other being. Our future evolution will be cultural. Leaving aside the hidebound, arrogant determinism explicit in such a statement, the frightful possibility is that they may be correct. Alone among the beings who have arisen on Earth, we have evolved into virtually total dependence upon not our nature but our nurture. We have lost the comfortably shifting experiential balance between the two that makes for healthy functioning beings in the world. We have chosen instead to gamble our future and the planet's on ideas.

This is risky. To place all of our chips on ideas is to deny any possible validity in our own biology. Our fanatical fixation on ideas (mind, reason, intellect, rationality — whatever you prefer) means that culturing has become more than just one useful aspect of being; it has become the human hyperspecialization.

It is possible to see our accumulated ideas, our ways of entertaining them, and our usual unquestioning dependence on both as together constituting an artificial replacement part, a fabricated *prosthetic device*. The prosthesis is a surrogate or substitute mode of approaching and apprehending the world. It has been fabricated through accumulating tradition to stand in the place of natural, biological, inherent ways of being,[6] those ways having been abrogated by the culturing process.

But the cultural prosthesis is not a mere whim, fancy, or conceit. It is necessary. Our physical and sociobehavioural evolution have brought us to a point at which we cannot do without it. We need it in order to function as social beings, in precisely the same way that animals we keep in domestication or captivity, for example, are dependent upon *us*. We will continue to need our supportive cultural prosthesis just as long as we persist in the denial

10

of our animalness, our biologic being. Our historic rejection of our own biology, which is commonly expressed as the human/Nature distinction, means that we require an artificial device to replace it.

The prosthesis is the "paradigm" — the set of beliefs, givens, and assumptions, the culturally conditioned perceptions and understandings of the world — that allows us to function as relatively peaceable social beings. It works very much as a filter does. It does not particularly matter what *sort* of filter it is, because these change over time. Any filter will do, but *none* will *not* do. Whether the artificial leg is of wood or plastic or aluminium does not really matter so long as it serves its supportive function. The specific content of the human cultural prosthesis does not particularly matter either. The brand is irrelevant so long as the problem, as it appears to be, is ideology.

Neil Evernden, the distinguished Canadian scholar in environmental thought, has observed that perhaps what most offends the humanistic establishment is modern ecosophy's challenge to ideology itself. It would seem that a basic human difficulty lies not in our need for some new ideology but rather our need for ideology, which can be supplied only by our prosthetic device. It seems that we need a surrogate appendage with which to attempt to offset the ontogenetically crippling psychological, social, and ecological effects of the condition in which we now find ourselves.

The overwhelming proportion of our thinking — governed as it is by ideology — is devoted to *technology*. (I am using the word in its broadest possible sense of a body of knowledge of how-to-do-it.) How-to-do-it, or technique, is the guts of human culturing. It matters not whether it is how to kill a chicken or how to change a tire or how to deal with a conundrum in logic or how to find human purpose and meaning in the cosmos. Or indeed how to predict, organize, and control a human society. "Technique refers to any complex of standardized means for attaining a pre-determined result."[7] Technique (and the knowledge thereof) is all.[8] The culturing (socially learned) activities of the various beings mentioned earlier — insects, birds, primates, cats — are technical, to be sure. They have to do with adjustments in the way they communicate, forage, or choose to laze about, but what they do not do is *dominate* the ways of life in which those beings remain. Their cultural innovations are kept in moderation.

Not so with us. The human animal has become a committed and confirmed specialist (and a uniquely gifted one) in learning, teaching, and applying techniques. In human societies, ways of doing have supplanted ways of being. It used to be said that the human primate became so successful (at least by the crass measure of reproductive success) because of all animals it emerged as the supreme generalist. It could and would eat almost anything, it possessed unprecedented sophistication in cooperative foraging, and it could live and prosper almost anywhere. All these things are true, undoubtedly, but they were achieved because of hyper-specialization. The human speciality is *storable, retrievable, transmissable technique*. We are bound to technique, indentured to technique, and we grew naturally into that serfdom along our evolutionary way. The dependence into which we have grown has made us not merely the servants of how-to-do-it, but one of it very artifacts. The problem animal is its own creation, its own domesticate.

PROSTHETIC
BEING

Human domestication is, nearly enough, a synonym for civilization. It is the quality of domesticatedness that has allowed us not only to be what we are but also to accomplish what we have on Earth in the course of our relatively brief tenure as a species. No wild animal of our size could possibly have achieved our level of world population, much less have tolerated our level of density, and no wild animal of any size could possibly have so transformed the face and function of the biosphere. Domestication confers special gifts, the most important of which is relative freedom from the pressure of natural selection, meaning at least temporary immunity to many normal ecological constraints. In return for these gifts, we have handed back, as it were, the quality of natural, integrated belongingness.

Among domesticated animals we are unique. All domesticated animals that are not human are our artifacts. We have created them by artificial selection — by choosing breeding stock to produce the particular features we desire. We, on the other hand, are *evolved* domesticates, the products of our own biological and cultural history. The qualities we now share with our living creations we developed over time on our own, without outside manipulative selection toward any preconceived pattern. Human uniqueness is even more profound than we have been taught to believe and to proclaim.

There are many visible earmarks of domestication. One, however, must be stressed above all others, and that is the matter of *dependence*. All domesticated animals depend for their day-to-day survival upon their owners. The capacities of wild self-sufficiency having long since been subtracted from them, they must depend upon whatever prosthetic devices their owners see fit to provide. The human domesticate has become equally dependent, not upon a proprietor, but upon storable, retrievable, transmissable technique. Technology provides us with everything we require. Knowledge of how-to-do-it sustains us utterly. And since none of us knows how to do *everything*, we are further dependent upon the expertise of countless others to provide even the most basic of daily necessities. Like that of a race horse or a Pekinese, our dependence upon agents external to ourselves is total. Without knowledge of how-to-do-it, or access to someone else who does know how, we are irretrievably helpless.

This is not merely a consequence of the complexity of modern technology. The human animal of any society and at any time was and is the creature of how-to-do-it. That is the most fundamental characteristic of humanness. Conceptualization and abstraction, instrumental reasoning, and their communication are our hallmarks. Everything else about us is secondary.

Domestication is a very strange state of being. A domesticated animal species is an evolutionary and ecological anomaly. It is not in the nature of any non-human being to arrive at such a condition by normal developmental process under free and wild circumstances. A domesticated animal is a human fabrication, arrived at after many generations of selective husbandry, its original progenitors having been taken from the wild into human custody.

To domesticate some non-human being, literally, is to bring it into our house. It is to amputate its wildness, to tame it; to train or otherwise coerce it into living with us and being of use to us; to make it part of our infrastructure. On a wider scale, we may see domestication as our forcing some accommodation to our wishes upon phenomena that are wild and not human. You can domesticate a plant by taking it home and causing it to grow around the house, and you can remove an entire forest or prairie so as to substitute domesticated plants and animals.

Although nowadays the planet fairly swarms with domesticated plants and animals, all of them actually come from relatively few original sources. Nearly all domesticated plants — grains and fruits and vegetables — are the hybrid progeny of strains that have been developed artificially by genetic manipulation. The wild precursors of these were very few. This is true of domesticated animals as well, although with the exception of the (sterile) mule, none to my knowledge is a cross between two discrete species. But even the animals spring from relatively few wild sources. There is one horse, one ox, one pig, one dog. Domesticated *breeds* are varieties, not hybrids; they freely reproduce.

(It is interesting that the wild antecedents of a number of our domesticated animals are either already extinct or on the edge of being so. The European wild horses and cattle are both long gone, for example, although zoo breeding from existing strains has produced facsimiles. And, as everyone knows, the final solution to the wolf "problem" is being prosecuted with undiminished zeal. It seems that we do not wish to be reminded of the original wildness of our household creatures. One cannot help wondering what *really* happened to *Homo sapiens neanderthalensis*, and to *H. erectus*, and to *H. habilis*, for that matter. Perhaps each, in its time, proved to be a family embarrassment. If you can't domesticate them, exterminate them.

Birds, although selectively bred, do not appear to have developed the same degree of dependence the domesticated mammals have. All "domesticated" birds are captives. Even chickens and turkeys would leave our premises if they were able, but selective breeding has sorely diminished or altogether removed their ability to fly. The tame parrot is caged or chained, and quite possibly wing-crippled. All aquarium fishes are captives, as are all other "exotic pets," and zoo animals.

While most birds seem to be forever testing their enclosures for escape routes, domestic mammals stay home as much by their own volition as by barricades. Often a horse will jump over its fence only to begin grazing where it landed. It seems the grass may have looked a little more appealing on the other side. Once the horse was over the fence, the choice of whether or not to leave was entirely its own. It elected to stay. It was restrained by its domesticity. By this I mean not only its generally low level of venturesomeness and confidence, and not only its need for company, but also its bond of dependence.

Domestication does not break this bond; it rearranges it. All of our domesticated mammals except the cat (a special case in all respects) are or were in Nature species with highly complex social organizations. Apart from the dog, all of them are hoofed herbivores. Cattle, camels, buffalo, horses, pigs, sheep, and goats live in the wild in relatively sophisticated societies of up to roughly 100 individuals. Typically, individual bonds are to the group, not to any physical place (home core). Within the group, each individual has a social place, and each is known to every individual.

Such places are defined only *in relation to* other members. The group is never so large that individual members do not know one another. Like the human family, the group functions as an entity interdependent with other groups and itself composed of interdependent individuals.

In the process of domestication the natural social organization is gradually broken down, and interdependence is transformed into unilateral dependence on the owner or proprietor. For the natural organization, which was maintained in the wild by a shifting web of lateral relationships, domestication substitutes a one-way flow of order, and the flow is downward, from above. In nature, group cohesiveness is maintained by mutualistic energetic bonds. In domestication, order is imposed from a linear, vertical hierarchy.

Ironically, perhaps, dependence on the one-way flow of order and control appears to be maintained not so much by the stockman or herder as by the animals themselves. The individual animals carry in their behavioural inheritance an unswerving drive toward social cohesiveness and complementarity. This inborn imperative has been called "the compulsion to comply."

In a state of nature, the glue that binds societies is compliance. The bond is especially strong because it is not one-way; it is mutual and interactive. As in the gravitational bond of solar systems, all sides contribute. Although it is not my intention to wound the sensibilities of the humanists, it must be said that the "human decency" for which we are so self-congratulatory is no invention of our own, but is the ancient "compulsion to comply," inherent in our biology. It is the basic prerequisite for any social order, and we carry it not in our cultures but in our genes. It is not taught or learned. It is there.

Some years ago, the popular media indulged in one of their familiar frenzies with accounts of human progenitors described as "killer apes," fiercely aggressive and highly dangerous territorial primates with an insatiable blood-lust.[1] This was patent rubbish. My faith in this is grounded, simply, in *Homo* the living animal and the sensate being. If we are biological products, then it is part of our nature to comply with one another toward the greater good of our social organization. One wonders why we do not do so, why we must be governed, from above, by hierarchical power structures.

Every zookeeper knows that there are strict upper limits to the number of captive wild animals that may safely (for them) be confined in a single enclosure. Naturally the number varies from species to species. But whatever the species, beyond a certain level of density, the inherent compulsion to comply breaks down, and violence can erupt. Probably the maximum number is not the same across an entire species. Likely it varies from population to population, or from group to group, depending on local environmental constraints or opportunities. In any case, there are always limits.

The strain created by crowding may be most severe among those species that are not only social, but also cooperative. These are animals who assume different tasks or roles in daily living. This list is relatively restricted. It appears not to include the hoofed animals, except elephants, but it does include wolves, coyotes and Cape hunting dogs, lions, hyenas, humans, baboons, chimpanzees and other primates, and probably at least some of the toothed whales and dolphins. Social cooperation involves such things as food sharing, food transport, babysitting, guarding, defending, teamwork in foraging and hunting (ambushes, relays, etc.), and so forth. For some reason, such species are especially sensitive to crowding. If you were to try to jam them in at cattle feed-lot density, you would have mayhem on your hands.

It is hypothesized here that the first unnaturally crowded cooperative social species was our own. It is to be emphasized again that the most barbaric punishment that can be visited upon such a species is dense confinement. The animal cannot cope with it; indeed, it is "designed" to *resist* it. It *must* resist it, in the interest of social survival and continuance. And so it was that when we ceased to depend on small-group gathering and hunting based from shifting, temporary home-sites, and began to settle down to a sedentary life of greater concentration in semi-permanent villages, that an enormously significant repression of our own nature took place.

It has been suggested that the Fall from Grace was the agricultural revolution. The expulsion from the Garden was the consequence of our having taken up gardening.[2] As human groupings expanded beyond the normal or natural upper limit for such cooperative primate societies, something had to be substituted for the inherent resistance to those densities. The compulsion to comply had been overwhelmed by numbers on more or less permanent sites. The solution, gradually arrived at, was institutionalized hierarchical governance. Power structures were an early component of the cultural prosthesis in sedentary human societies. The one-way downward flow of externally imposed order slowly but inexorably replaced lateral mutuality. The upright primate had entered permanent domestic servitude.[3]

But what a very strange thing to have happened. No other animal had entered domesticity on its own. Why us? For the species to even *begin* to enter such an unprecedented way of life, it must have been predisposed ("preadapted") to do so. Not that there was intent involved, but the species had to have certain pre-existing anatomical, physiological, behavioural, and psychological qualities to allow the process even to start.

Domesticated mammal species have a number of characteristics in common. This is no accident. We observe certain desirable

traits in individual animals, then select those individuals for breeding purposes, thus perpetuating and intensifying the occurrence
of those useful qualities. In some breeds, such as dairy cattle,
breeding techniques have become so sophisticated that results are
comfortably predictable almost without exception.

The domesticate must not have a mind, or a will, of its own.
It must totally rely on its master for food, drink, shelter, fresh air,
exercise, and information. Such sensory stimulation as it may
receive, including sex, is also largely determined by its captor, who
decides whether or not to afford the animal even the company of
its own species. Dependence is virtually absolute. Security is given.
The domesticate need no longer be able even to detect danger,
much less escape, still less defend itself.

Docility and tractability are almost as important as dependence, although when some extra measure of control is required
for a chronically recalcitrant individual, we have our ways. Most
domesticates readily accept the downward flow of command. Few
are dangerous. It used to be said that the domestic Jersey bull was
the most dangerous non-human being on Earth. But Jerseys have
declined in popularity because they are not high-volume produc-
ers, and there are fewer bulls of any breed around nowadays in
any case. Most of those that do remain (of dairy breeds at least)
tend to stay shut up in their laboratory stalls for semen drawing.
There is not much to fear from any domesticated mammal of
whatever size; little or no spirit of self-defence is left in any of
them.

The ancestors of our domesticated hoofed animals had the
highly desirable characteristic of not being bound to a physical
home base, or a "core" range. They moved about pretty well constantly, and thus lacked the attachment-to-place that is so evident
in more sedentary species. They could fare equally well anyplace,
within reasonable climatic and other ecological limits. Interestingly

enough, most domestic animal ancestors were relatively large, lived in open or montane habitats, and were non-selective feeders.[4] So were ours. The domesticate is almost infinitely transferable.

Most if not all hoofed animals in the wild have quite well-developed interdependent social structures. Group organization varies widely according to species, and according to the ecology of each species, but all have social arrangements of subtlety and sensitivity. Across a herd of zebras or antelopes, *aliveness and sensitivity* fairly sparkle back and forth, in a crackling-quick communication network shared by all. In the interest of their predictability and controllability under domestication, animals must be caused to abandon and forget their ancient interpersonal relationships, and this we have accomplished. Social interaction in a herd of cattle, save for the ephemeral cow–calf relationship, is negligible. The only bond that is evident is one of dependence on whoever fills the feed bucket and water trough.

Farm animals show a high level of "followership." This should not be surprising, for they were in Nature notably gregarious. (This is not to imply that in the wild there was "leadership," for this I very much doubt.) This inclination to group cohesion was no doubt much prized by early human domesticators, who took full advantage of it. The herd or flock that sticks together is quite ridiculously easy to manipulate.

Hoofed domesticates as a whole demonstrate tolerance worthy of a Job to both physical and psychological maltreatment. They show no particular sign of frustration, discomfort, or anxiety, even under the most appalling deprivation. Carrying in their pre-domestic inheritance the inclination to live in large groups, they might be expected to endure somewhat more crowding than, say, wolves or baboons possibly could. But even naturally gregarious animals such as cattle are called upon to suffer a degree

21

of mutual proximity in confinement that could not possibly occur in the wild. Imagine, if you can, a herd of Cape buffalo compressed as tightly as beef cattle commonly are; the immediate consequence would be nightmarish, to put it mildly. Also, our farm animals seem not to be unduly disturbed by confinement itself. A large measure of the life of a dairy cow is spent standing in an individual stall, yet she lives, and lives, and continues to produce. Her tolerance of enclosure is staggering.

Extraordinary also, is the domesticate's acceptance of a remarkable level of sameness, or homogeneity, in its living environment. There is little or no change, from hour to hour, day to day, year to year, in the domesticate's universe of sight, sound, scent, taste, or tactility. All remains exactly the same. Remember this the next time you see a deer tasting the wind, sampling the sound spectrum, checking the littlest details of its visible surround. Try to imagine the scope of its sensory environment. Luckily for the jailed victims of experiential deprivation, most domesticates have dramatically reduced sensory acuity by comparison with that of their wild relatives. Even so, they are alive, and they have sense receptors, which, blunted or not, must still yearn for *something* in the way of stimulation. But nothing comes in. Nothing. Still, they live, and are fruitful, and multiply.

A major influence on our selection of domesticates for breeding is their fecundity. We want them to be fast and prolific multipliers. Whereas most wild animals have well-defined breeding times, usually tied to food availability for the young according to the seasons, domesticates mate the year round. They have utterly lost sensitivity to natural environmental cycles.

For those of us who breed high-priced cattle such as Holsteins, however, even "normal" domesticated productivity is insufficient, and nowadays one valuable cow may be caused to provide several or even many progeny from one oestrus. Superovulation (the production of a number of eggs) is induced with drugs. The eggs are then fertilized by the injection of the most expensive blue-ribbon semen. (The value of the semen is determined by the productivity of a bull's female offspring.) The resulting embryos are then flushed from the "donor" and implanted in cows of lesser value who have been chemically prepared to receive them, and will act as surrogate mothers in bringing the calves to term. The recent emergence of human "reproductive clinics" has been made possible through methods perfected with animal "models."

However and whenever conceived, however, young domesticated animals never really *grow up*. The period of infantility is prolonged through the duration of the individual's lifetime. This is of the greatest importance to the proprietor. The last thing we want is our domesticates reaching *social* maturity, because that would mean their recovery of mutuality and interdependence, and the dissolution of their bond of dependence on us. So we select for animals who never develop the mature social graces of wildness.

On the other hand, it is critically important that the animals develop as rapidly as possible physically. We can countenance no delay in the transformation of feed into meat, whether for the abattoir or the milking barns. Careful selection of breeding stock has accomplished both desiderata. We now produce animals of arrested social development who grow like beanstalks, who retain the docility of immaturity while coming to physical (including sexual) maturity at a furious rate. Even adults, by comparison with their wild counterparts, have a babyish look about them. They are rounder in outline, with relatively larger heads and eyes, softer facial features, and a decidedly wimpish and unathletic demeanour. But they are big.

Again by comparison with their wild counterparts, our domesticates are conspicuously precocious sexually. Dairy farmers will breed young heifers when they are barely more than calves. A female Alaskan malamute in my household came into heat when she was only six months old; a five-month-old male pup tried to mate with her. Wolves, we are told, do not show sexual urgings until they are almost two years old.[5] Also, dogs are notably promiscuous, wolves much less so, and in "ideal" pack situations, possibly not at all.

As the result of selective breeding, domesticated animals have become extraordinarily varied. The difference between a Chihuahua and an Irish wolfhound is even greater than that between a pygmy and a Sumo wrestler. It was the astonishing variety in the appearance of fancy pigeon breeds, all descended from a common ancestor, that gave Charles Darwin a vital insight into the enormous potential of biological radiation. Just as intriguing is the fact that distinct *behavioural* characteristics develop in the various breeds, and members of a distinct breed (or race) tend to become more and more like one another. Individuality tends to diminish; predictability (and thus controllability) is thereby enhanced.

There seems to be in domesticated animals, especially perhaps cattle, a reduced ability to communicate among themselves. This may be a result of both the deterioration of the social structure and reduced sensory acuity, or indeed it may be one of the causes. More likely, the three phenomena evolved together, in feedback fashion, over the thousands of generations of captive procreation. With group social organization and individual social place long since gone, what you see in the cattle feed-lot is all that remains. Glazed, dulled, blurred travesties of their once-wild ancestors, they give the impression not only of failure to recognize one another, but of failure to recognize even their own species. But they still have sense receptors of some kind. They also still have central nervous systems. (That they may no longer be able to articulate or even grossly demonstrate their stress and discomfort, it must be said, can scarcely be justification for the manner in which they are so unrelentingly and callously maltreated.)

Having in mind the grotesquely reduced and distorted physical, physiological, and behavioural qualities of most domestic animals, it is not surprising that they have become ecological misfits. As individual place has been lost in the herd, and as the herd has ceased to be a society, so too has vanished the ecological place of the species itself. A domesticated hoofed grazer or browser no longer has relevance in the broader natural community. It is in every respect a "loose cannon," contributing nothing to the functioning of the greater living surround, and potentially devastating to it.

Such animals, so deficient in the ability even to communicate among themselves, appear to have also lost all trace of sensitivity to *inter*species information exchange. Wild animals are good naturalists; they know what is going on in their communities. They are "tuned in" on all frequencies at all times. Just as the freeloaders know when it is time to take advantage of a lion kill, or the gulls and terns know when the fishing squadrons of white pelicans are successful, everyone in a greater wild society knows and benefits from knowledge of what everyone else is up to. Predator and prey will communicate an instant before the decisive act.[6] Birds and small mammals of many species will set up a hue and cry at the appearance of a predator, and no one has any difficulty understanding the content of the message. I am confident that there are many other, much more subtle interspecies information networks. Domesticates are not party to them, and go their blundering way as best they can.

Among domesticates the dog is a separate study, and not merely because dogs are usually household companions. Dogs are the only domesticated non-human animals descended from socially *cooperative* ancestors. Unlike the vegetarian grazers and browsers, they have in their biological inheritance the memory of *contrib-utory* participation in a close-knit family-centred group.

There was some debate among scientists at one point over the identity of the wild dog ancestor. Konrad Lorenz, one of the founders of modern ethology, claimed that almost all dogs are descended from the golden jackal (*Canis aureus*), with some having a small subsequent post-domestication admixture of wolf (*C. lupus*) blood. "The purest wolf-dogs that exist are certain breeds of Arctic America, particularly the so-called malemutes, huskies, etc."[7] Most authorities today have rejected the jackal hypothesis in favour of the wolf, which at one time lived almost throughout Europe, northern and central Asia, and most of North America.[8] Although the domestic dog has been dignified with its own scientific name (*C. familiaris*), it will breed successfully with both wolves and coyotes (*C. latrans*), producing fertile offspring.

The profound differences between the wolf/coyote/dog social organization and that of the hoofed domesticates would indicate that the first domesticated canid of whatever species was not placed in incarceration, as the cattle were, but became an integrated member of human society very quickly. Perhaps these earliest familiars were not quite so attractive in adulthood as they were in puppyhood (there are uneven reports about the behaviour of "pet" wolves and wolf-dog crosses in maturity), but over time the prolonged infantility of domestication began to produce more docile, tractable, friendly (dependent) animals.

The dog, no matter how long domesticated, retains a powerful need for social companionship and integration within a closed (family) group. Since its compulsion is not merely to comply, but also to cooperate, it is of all non-primates by far the easiest to teach and the quickest to learn.[9] The old nostrum about dogs being "anxious to please" sounds soft and somewhat sappy, to be sure, but there is no doubt that the dog is predisposed to do its bit in group affairs. The "tricks" to which so many dogs are subjected are demeaning, insulting, and human power-and dominance-tainted, but they clearly illustrate the point. Although some of the demands we make upon them are more frivolous than others, dogs *are* motivated to participate, and to do what they are called upon to do in the greater interest. No other non-human domesticate has this inherent quality.

The domesticated mammal is not a hybrid. It is docile, tractable, predictable, and controllable. Initially it may be smaller, but may become somewhat larger than its wild antecedents. It grows very rapidly, but even into maturity retains many infantile characteristics both physical and behavioural. It is dependent on us. It is sexually precocious and promiscuous. There may be great variability in appearance, but behavioural individuality is low. There is pronounced reduction in sensory acuity and the ability to communicate both intra- and interspecifically. Dogs excepted, social behaviour is much simplified and low in subtlety. Dogs excepted again, there is no attachment to physical place, and no awareness of social place. No domesticate has an ecologic place.[10]

Non-human animals with these features are the products of selective breeding. Humans are not; they are the products of evolutionary process. It used to be thought that the human animal, big brain and all, burst upon the world with spectacular suddenness. Surely it would take eons of time for natural selection to produce a being with such extraordinary qualities. But as it appears, there was plenty of time.

The genus *Homo* has been around for at least two million years, and perhaps a good deal longer than that. Analysis of ancient skulls, for example, puts dates of three million years on brains that are much more like ours, much less like those of apes. As the Kenyan palaeontologist-conservationist Richard Leakey and the science writer Roger Lewin have pointed out, whatever evolutionary factors actually produced the human brain, they had been at work long enough to have shaped the basic pattern by at least three million years ago. They say, "by two million years ago, divergence in gross brain organization is apparent between *Homo* and *Australopithecus*: in *Homo*, the temporal and frontal lobes are becoming enlarged, indicating the powerful evolutionary forces at work during this period, steadily enhancing the humanness of our ancestral brains."[11] Even haphazard natural selection can do a great deal in such a span of time. Our artificially selected cattle go back perhaps six or seven thousand years. The Dobermann pinscher was not even a gleam in anyone's eye 150 years ago. Geneticists crank out fruit flies by the hour. A lot can happen in years measured by the millions.

Let us turn now to culturing. In prehistory the first natural phenomenon to be used by human progenitors toward its eventual domestication was neither a wolf puppy nor a wild geranium, but a chemical process — fire. Hundreds of thousands of years before the beginning of the husbandry of animals and plants, fire began to be tamed, and trained to live with us. Very much later it was brought into our house and installed there, at our beck and call.

Fire was no ordinary technology. How-to-do-it had been part of the human and protohuman culturing story, most probably, since before our ancestors would have been recognizable as hominids. Primate cooperative techniques of foraging, alarm and defence, nightly nesting, and so on, had been with us "forever." Long before there was the most elementary spoken language, the knowledge of how to do certain things was learned by observation, as it is by modern non-human primates. Much later, the social storing, retrieving, and transmitting of technical behaviour allowed the development and refinement of the earliest tools and weapons. (The distinction is difficult. Some anthropologists hold that if a rock is used to hammer other rocks, or to hammer prey animals, then it is a tool; if it is used to hammer others of one's own species, it is a weapon. We shall not pursue that further here, provocative though it is.)

Fire is qualitatively different. You don't pick it up and hit something or someone with it — at least not usually. You cannot eat it and you cannot store it — at least not with early or prehuman technical capacity. Fire requires a degree of abstraction to be used in any way other than for immediate warmth or light. It takes at least some time for a fire to grow, to cook something, or to remove a forest copse. The use of fire requires sophisticated concepts of cause-and-effect. And it is very demanding technically. Given that you have experienced some of its utility, you then have to learn how to feed it, how to keep it and control it, how to transport it, and much later, how to make it — from scratch.

We will probably never know exactly how long fire has been part of the human experience. Half a million years ago (about half a million years before the domestication of animals and plants) *Homo erectus* in China was cooking regularly. There are *H. erectus* hearths and fire pits in France of twice that age. Whether the latter were used for cooking we cannot yet know, but one million years is about twice as long ago as the emergence of the earliest (Neanderthal) *H. sapiens*. There has been discovered in northern Kenya an apparent hearth that dates to two and one half million years.[12] At that time there was a species of human around, *H. habilis* the handyman, but there also seem to have been at least two sorts of australopithecines still extant, perhaps more. No one yet knows to whom the hearth, if it is one, may have belonged.

One may quite comfortably speculate that it was used by somebody in the human lineage. The use (not the control) of fire is ancient. Many animals seem to be fascinated by fire, and readily approach it. Some birds attend natural grass fires in order to pick up small creatures attempting to escape. Other birds use embers with which to dress their feathers. There is in the Philippines a little primate relative of ours, *Tarsier syrichta*, which used to be called *T. carbonarius* for its custom of fiddling about with live coals at camp fires. On this and related evidence, it should not really surprise us if the very early hominids, and even their ancestors, were well acquainted with at least some of the virtues of fire, ten or a dozen million years ago.

It is not difficult to picture a family-centred group of social primates huddled at night about a fire, with their excellent daylight vision diminished by its glare, glancing furtively and with apprehension into the blackness beyond. Night is not the best time for any terrestrial primate; for one with burgeoning powers of abstraction, fear of the unseeable may have been an early cost of the benefit of the technology of warmth and illumination. There may have been a concomitant dawning of the concept of "otherness" — we, here in the light of the flames, that, out there, in the void beyond. Fear and dread of the "other" which is Nature may have longer roots than we customarily choose to believe.

Whenever it was that fire was brought under control, that control must have been something of a morale builder.[13] It may have given rise to the first faint sensation of the Faustian and wholly unnatural idea of *power*, and this may well have taken place earlier rather than later in our evolutionary history. Controllable fire may have contributed to the reducing of the twelve-hour equatorial darkness, and thus sleep, to the eight hours or less we really seem to need. Four extra hours for eating, for tool making and maintenance, for sex, for communication, for tradition making, for language, for ideas.[14]

And, some authors say, for social bonding. I think not. As we have seen, social bonding is *there*, in the very bone marrow of beings like these. They were tied together socially long before they used fire. This is not to say that a "bond" did not develop, but it was of a totally different kind. It was the bond of dependence on knowledge. Individuals were already interdependent in their social organization. As a group they became dependent on fire technology. They became dependent on how-to-do-fire.

These highly social and cooperative primates had long been specialists in how to do things, especially tools and weapons, as well as how to do essential behavioural things, and they had become increasingly dependent upon that knowledge. But up until this point, none of their dependence was on anything *external* to themselves. Social behaviour is internal to oneself; tools and weapons are extensions of oneself, carried in the hand. Fire is foreign; it is a qualitative jump beyond primate how-to knowledge.

The domesticator of our ancestors was this intensification of their dependence on technical knowledge beyond anything previously experienced. It was a difference in kind. Although through all the millennia of gathering and hunting there was individual interdependence in the group (there still is), some of our reliance gradually shifted away from the collective toward non-mutualistic unilateral dependence on skills and knowledge. The patterned how-to of much more sophisticated tools and weapons, strategic defence and hunting, cooking, shelter construction, and so on. And eventually the how-to of the raising of plants and animals in captivity, and perhaps most important of all for its future implications, the how-to of artificial ("prosthetic") human social organization and control.

But by the time we got around to the politics of power structures, we had long since evolved, quite naturally, into our modern anatomical, physiological, and behavioural form. Over countless generations, natural selection had favoured a brain specializing in vision, conceptualization, and abstraction, and a body to go with it, having, as it were, discarded as unnecessary the formidable physical equipment of our closest relatives. Whoever first cradled an orphaned wolf puppy was indistinguishable from you or me.

There are two domesticated carnivores — the dog and the cat — and assorted single- and cloven-hoofed herbivores, but only one primate has entered the unique and restricted realm of domesticity. That we were the first such biological phenomenon ever to arise out of any phylogenetic crucible allowed us, as it were, to use our own species as template for the manufacture of subsequent non-human artifacts in the human image, or at least a good working facsimile thereof.

The human species is a large bipedal terrestrial primate. Our physical demeanour, by comparison with that of other large primates, suggests a developmental stage somewhere between infantility and immaturity — relatively large head and eyes, soft features, weak jaws, small teeth, frail physique. The size of the skull necessitates somewhat "premature" birth of the human baby, which in turn results in unusually prolonged infancy by comparison with that of our closest relatives. The period of childhood is proportionately longer.

Since our closest living relative is the chimpanzee, a comparison is in order here. A chimp's gestation period is just about the same as ours. But our period of infancy is twice as long (six as opposed to three years), our juvenile phase is twice as long (fourteen as against seven years), and as adults we live at least twice as long, usually longer. Female chimpanzees come to sexual maturity at about nine years of age, which on the same comparative scale would have the human menarche at eighteen, whereas in fact it occurs between ten and fourteen. As one might expect, the domesticated primate is sexually precocious.

Promiscuity, characteristic of domesticates, may have received an extra boost from our primate genes. Chimpanzees are famous-

ly promiscuous, gorillas less so. And of course year-round sexual activity in the human female is another badge of the domesticated condition.[15] We need not dwell here on human fecundity.

Reduced sensory acuity, common to all domesticates, plagues
us daily whether we are conscious of it or not. Although we do
have primate stereoscopic vision, our eyesight is not otherwise
notable, and the rest of our sensory apparatus is sorely reduced.
Our hearing is pathetically diminished, our olfactory range and
sensitivity, by comparison with those of other mammals, virtually non-existent. Our taste discrimination appears to be relatively
poor. Our primate tactility and hand–eye coordination are, of
course, our specialties, and on these rests most of our sensory
reliance.

Our sensory inadequacies, ironically enough, probably assist
us in enduring the terrible dreary sameness and homogeneity of
the human physical environment, and our crowded confinement
within it. Our tolerance of sensory undernutrition and our placid,
docile acceptance of it is worthy of that paragon of passivity, the
Holstein cow.

As it is with other domesticates, our identities seem not to be
strongly attached or bonded to any physical site. In any modern
city, homogeneous stands of identical apartment houses, condominiums, row houses, town houses, and suburban boxes, with
their identical interiors, bespeak placelessness, rootlessness, and
minimal individuality. We willingly pick up stakes and move; the
new site, most probably, will be an inorganic fabrication indistinguishable in any environmental sense from the one we left.
Although we may take our domestic pets with us, our estrange-
ment from wild non-human Nature will continue uninterrupted.

Our high degree of domesticated followership, obvious in a St.
Peter's Square or a Nuremberg rally, may also underlie the phenomenon of "trendiness," whether in residential neighbourhoods,

restaurants, television culture, or social criticism. Anyone who has ever endured life in the military knows about committed followership and knee-jerk obedience, as no doubt does anyone who has ever served a political master. In our role as domesticates, both our individual and collective docility and tractability have consuming importance.

Lock-step followership is deeply rooted in us, if not to "leaders," who do, after all, come and go, but to doctrines. As Arthur Koestler (following the American philosopher William James and others) points out, either through social integration or some "peak experience" the individual human seemingly must acquire some self-transcending structure of belief. This, it will be clear, is what I refer to as the ideological prosthesis. Koestler notes, however, that

> *once they become institutionalised as the collective property of a group, they degenerate into rigid doctrines which, without losing their emotive appeal to the true believer, potentially offend his reasoning faculties [causing a split between emotion and intellect].... To eliminate this dissonance, various forms of double-think have been designed at various times — powerful techniques of self-deception, some crude, some extremely sophisticated.*[16]

This is a critical element in the process and maintenance of our domestication. The role of self-deceit in prevailing human ideologies I shall come to later.

It was pointed out earlier in this chapter that domesticated animals, especially cattle, appear to have lost very much of their communicative ability. This misfortune has clearly not befallen the socially cooperative domesticates. Both dogs and ourselves retain powers of communication which for breadth, depth, and subtlety are unequalled in the domesticated community. It is very possible that intraspecific communication has been strongly selected *against* in the breeding of hoofed animals, as one measure in the desired breakdown of their social structure. We did not want to do that with dogs, and perhaps could not. In the human case, communication — especially of abstract information — is the major linchpin of the species. Without it there would be no human to talk about. No doubt communicative abilities are related to the great difference in domesticated social maturing between hoofed animals, on the one hand, dogs and people, on the other.

Utter dependence is common to all domesticates. Non-human species depend wholly on us; we depend wholly on storable, retrievable, transmissible technique. But although dependence is a useful descriptive criterion for the domesticated animal, in the affairs of the world of natural wildness the overwhelming importance of the domesticate is its ecological placelessness. We humans and our domesticated artifacts, alien misfits that all of us are, have profoundly and perhaps irretrievably changed both the form and the functioning of the ecosphere. How we have achieved that is the burden of the following chapter.

THE
EXOTIC
TRANSPLANTS

Alone among domesticated animals, the human species is not the product of the artificial selection of breeding stock. We are what we are as the result of natural evolutionary process. There are many claims to human uniqueness, some more persuasive than others,[1] to which may be added our innate, inherent domesticity, with all the characteristics that that implies. One feature of the domesticated condition is of particular importance: the absence of ecologic place for the species, its separation[2] from Nature. Indeed, were it not for human domestication there would *be* no "Nature," no "other," no concept of wildness. There would be no one and no reason to conceive of them.

Domesticated species have become placeless "exotics" foreign to every natural community in the world. In an ecologic sense they belong nowhere, but in practice, given the right conditions, they can prosper almost anywhere, often at great cost to native plants and animals, their relationships, and their communities. They seem to do best when introduced to areas already significantly disturbed by human settlement. However, this is a consequence not only of their domesticity, but also of their sheer exoticness. Many *wild* animals, transferred to new situations, have had similar effects.

Obviously plants and animals have been moving from place to place, exploring new areas, since life emerged, The entire evolutionary story has been one of plasticity and change, with endless probing, venturing, and testing of old and new environments in usually old and conservative but sometimes new and radical ways. The break-up of the protocontinents, the emergence of islands and archipelagos, the changes in climatic regimes over a thousand million years, permitted not only the appearance of new forms of plant and animal life but also the dispersal of those forms over areas previously uninhabited by them.

Clearly there must have been profound ecological transformations as new species — whole new faunas and floras — evolved. At times such changes may well have been tumultuous. In general, however, most of these dispersals of faunas and floras took place so gradually and over such immense spans of time that few if any of them would have been visible on any mortal calendar. Natural evolutionary process (micro-organisms excepted) is deliberation itself.

Some ecological processes, on the other hand, can be rapid. The most familiar example would be the reoccupation of the land following the retreat of the most recent ice sheet. Plants and animals followed the meltback with (for Nature) extraordinary speed. New communities developed almost instantaneously, from a geological point of view. Even faster is the recovery of a forest community following fire, or hurricane, or pruning by insects. Sometimes the original community returns on site; sometimes a series of stages, each consisting of a different set of species, fol-

lows. The transformation of the African savannah at the onset of
the rainy season appears nothing short of miraculous.

Such events, however, are normal and (perhaps even the ice)
roughly cyclic. Sometimes a foreign species may find its way into
a new (to it) natural community and make its effect felt very quickly. These events are usually characterized as "invasions," and
although some of them are natural, most are not. There is a sorry,
dreary, and extended list of biological disruptions and disasters
resulting from the introduction of exotic species to new and foreign areas by people. Much has been written about this phenomenon, but the benchmark contribution was made by the British
ecologist Charles Elton thirty years ago.[3] Noting the long prehistoric period of the mixing and remixing of floras and faunas,
Elton observed that "we are artificially stepping up the whole
business.... We must make no mistake: we are seeing one of the
great historical convulsions in the world's fauna and flora."[4] The
present convulsion is entirely the work of our species.

There are two sorts of human-induced exotic introductions:
inadvertent and deliberate. The first, unintentional series, began
hundreds of years ago with early intercontinental travel by sea,
and continues today by all the modern means of transport. This
list consists mostly of small beasties who stow away with us unnoticed — uncountable pathogens, parasites, and other micro-organisms; a multitude of invertebrates, house mice, and ships' rats. It
would be difficult to imagine that any of these was transported
with conscious intent; the human travellers were no more fond
of them than were the eventual recipients. The catastrophic effect
of imported European diseases on native North American people
is well known. Familiar too has been the crop devastation wrought
around the world by accidentally transported herbivorous insects.
A current example of inadvertent transport — but only one among
thousands — is that of hordes of tiny European zebra mussels

now infesting the Great Lakes, having arrived there by way of the ballast tanks of ocean-going freighters. I have heard reports of hundreds of thousands of mussels per square metre.

But these shipments are, after all, unintentional. International screenings, inspections, quarantines, etc., do what they can nowadays to keep the lid on these massive dispersals of unwanted and dangerous mini-travellers, but everyone knows the process of intercontinental introduction to be planet-wide, and accelerating. There is abroad in the biosphere a growing, creeping and crawling *sameness* that is the utter antithesis of ecological and evolutionary process. The natural singularity and unique identity of the several continents are fast dissolving; it is becoming one homogeneous world. And not only that: by virtue of the increasing numbers of the same familiar roster of humans and their satellites, and the concomitant fragmentation and extirpation of indigenous faunas, world communities are becoming *simpler* as well. Nature thrives on diversity and variety, multiplicity of forms and functions; anything that tends to reduce the normal complexity of interrelationships is biologically destructive. (Sameness and simplicity are among the more obvious hallmarks of domestication.)

The accidental relocation of undesirables is one thing, but the deliberate infection of a natural community with foreign elements is another. Until quite recently, it was the wont of civilized folk the world over to attempt to improve upon Nature by adding ornamental enhancement brought with them in cages from afar. Thus were the house sparrow (1850 to 1867) and the common starling (1890) visited upon North America, having initially been released by their admirers in Brooklyn and New York City, respectively. Both have blanketed almost the entire settled portion of the continent, and have made strong beach-heads in the West Indies and elsewhere. Their contributions, like those of so many invaders, have been difficult to detect. Of the house sparrow,

ornithologist Earl Godfrey says, "It is a pugnacious ruffian, driving away our native birds and usurping their nesting cavities."[5]
The starling similarly uses nesting holes at the expense of some
indigenous species. Neither, however, appears to have had truly
grievous effect. For destructiveness they have not been in the same
league with agriculture and urbanization.[6]

Although both the sparrow and the starling now number in
the hundreds of millions in their new hemisphere, their disrup-
tive interspecies accomplishments pale beside those of the infa-
mous European rabbits in Australia. Introduced in Victoria in
1859, the animals instantly established themselves, and their sto-
ried reproductive prowess took over from there. Between 1880
and 1886 they "traversed New South Wales at an average rate of
seventy miles a year.... The impact of the rabbit was catastrophic. Country that had supported lush grass was now eaten down
until it resembled a bowling green. At times of drought the rabbits died by the millions, but before doing so they ring-barked
and killed shrubs and bushes, and ate grass down to its roots."[7]

The plague continued relatively unchecked until the 1950s,
when some measure of rabbit control was achieved with the introduction of myxomatosis, a virus disease. Although it enjoyed spectacular success in the early stages, removing 98 percent of the
rabbits when it first struck, "the second epidemic produced only
85 per cent mortality. With each succeeding epidemic there was
a reduction in the success rate until the sixth epidemic only killed
25 per cent of the remaining rabbits. The virus still takes its toll,
but is now less effective than ever."[8] The rabbits are still there,
and no doubt always will be.

At the height of the infestation, someone calculated a total population of rabbits in Australia of 750 million, "between them eating as much as 100 million sheep."[9] The rabbit scourge was an
immediate economic disaster for many herders, and for the coun-

try. However, its ecological impact, in terms of indigenous Australian wildlife, was not fully appreciated until later, when it was noticed that several grassland-adapted marsupials and a number of birds had vanished. Some had succumbed to anti-rabbit poisoning programs, others to the devastation of their habitat by the intruders.

There are several reasons for the spectacular success of the European rabbit in Australia (as well as New Zealand and many other islands). It encountered ideal climate and habitat. Ecologically, the new situation was made to order. There was virtually no pressure from predation. Neither the feral dingo dog (thought to have been brought as a domesticate by the early settling Aborigines) nor the European fox (imported for the traditional British hunt) could make a dent in the rabbit populations. Although there are a few native carnivorous marsupials, none was up to this task. Nor were the birds of prey or the large reptiles. The wide spectrum of native marsupial mammals could not begin to match the invader's reproduction. The rabbit simply took over a community that had no prior experience of it and no defences against it. Australia's native fauna and flora had developed no "antibody," no "immunity," no resistance to an exotic plague.

In New Zealand, parts of which were as inundated with rabbits as southeast Australia, various stratagems were employed against the infestation, the most noteworthy of which was the introduction of large numbers of several species of weasel. Not only did these fail to accomplish much in the way of rabbit control, but they also turned their attention to native birds and reptiles, whose numbers they sorely reduced. New Zealand's unique native vegetation has also been extensively — in some places, irreparably — damaged by the appetites of at least seven species of exotic deer,[10] as well as the thar (an alpine goat)[11] and chamois. All of these large herbivores found total freedom from natural predation in their new habitat. It is worth noting that of the fifty or so exotic species now resident in New Zealand, more than half have no natural predators at all.[12]

We rarely notice the *presence* of predators. In healthy situations predators have little or no effect on populations of prey species. The two have struck a balance, as it were, and predator numbers tend to follow the fortunes of their prey. Usually, predators are but one of a number of governors, or controls, which act together to maintain population levels. But in those cases where the prey animals have not co-evolved with predators they may lack the ability to rebound reproductively from the new pressure. Or, a species might have evolved in a mutually beneficial relationship with, for example, flying predators such as gulls, hawks, or owls, but be entirely innocent of and vulnerable to terrestrial ones such as rats, weasels, or mongooses. To their ultimate cost, this has been the experience of many bird species on oceanic islands.

Obviously rats have overrun the planet because of their skill in stowing away in human shipping. But there is more to it than that. Rats are omnivorous; they will readily eat animal and plant material of virtually any sort. This flexibility in food preferences is matched by extraordinary adaptiveness. Given a half-decent climate, rats can live almost everywhere. They are superb generalists. It is no accident that their world distribution coincides with our own. I should not be a bit surprised to learn that they have joined us in year-round outposts in Antarctica.

Rats have infested the sugar cane plantations of the West Indies for some 350 years. Various and sundry control agents were experimented with, to no visible avail, until the nineteenth-century introduction of the small Indian mongoose. This versatile little carnivore went to work on the rats with alacrity, and excellent results were evident almost immediately after its introduction to Jamaica. Mongooses were subsequently established, before the turn of this century, in Grenada, Barbados, Cuba, Puerto Rico, Trinidad, and

Hispaniola, and by the mid-twentieth century they had reached pretty well all of the Caribbean islands.[13] They continue to do a reasonably satisfactory, if no longer spectacular, job of rat catching.

There was only one problem. The mongoose, according to Clive Roots, is "the complete omnivore, and eats whatever it can find."[14] Rats are well known to defend themselves with vigour and effectiveness, and will band together in formidable array when the occasion demands. Mongooses are also well known to turn to many kinds of birds, reptiles, amphibians, and insects as available. And although they seem to prefer animal food, they will readily eat fruits, and perhaps other plant products as well. The point is that the mongoose does not distinguish between the rats it is supposed to devour and the vulnerable native birds and other small animals who are a great deal easier to catch. A long list of endemic island species has been destroyed in the West Indies, Hawaii, and many other places by the mongoose. And the flexible, versatile rats persist. It is possible that at least in some places the rats and mongooses may have arrived at a semi-natural "equilibrium."

The worldwide dispersal of the rat, and of so many lesser fry such as disease vectors of all sorts, was never intended by anyone. The dispersal of thousands of kinds of undesirables was part of the price of doing business — one of those unavoidable "externalities" that accompanied the intercontinental human venture. And it is by no means over. There is simply no way we could guarantee the containment of, for example, the organisms of plant and animal (including human) diseases today. That, we — and the millions of other species in the world — must live and die with. There is no going back to continental ecologic integrity.

Nor, sad to say, is there any possibility of retrieving or recalling the wild plant and animal species we have *deliberately* introduced the world over. We have consciously dispersed hundreds of exotic species to every point of the compass. Some of our efforts have failed utterly; some failed initially, but after repeated attempts the transplants "took." Scores of endemic species have given way before them, powerless to survive the onslaught. The devastation wrought in places such as Australia and New Zealand, in the Hawaiian Islands, in Fiji, and in scores of other islands, as well as on continental masses, is not now recoverable. The deed is done.[15]

Unfortunately there is yet more. As it turns out, the ecological horrors brought about by inadvertently and deliberately introduced wild animals and plants are fairly small beer by comparison with the effects of transplanted domesticated species. This list is much shorter. Among the animals, we have cattle, sheep and goats, swine, horses and donkeys, dogs, and cats. The late Peter Scott used to call these ubiquitous human satellites "the wrecking crew." Wherever they go, domesticated animals are sorry news for indigenous biotas. Even when safely secured behind fences, they are an enormous drain on the natural productivity of the land that must subsidize them, to the cost of native species that must be sustained by the same natural processes. And they (sheep and cattle, for example) take up space — lots of it — removing vital and irreplaceable habitat for countless wild plant and animal communities thus dispossessed.

But that is only part of the story. From time to time, our domesticated creatures have a way of escaping. Even worse, from time to time we have a way of turning them loose to fend for themselves. As often as not, they perish. Unfortunately, sometimes they find conditions to their liking — agreeable climate and abundant food, absence of disease and predators, and so on. Occasionally they find a veritable terrestrial paradise in which to thrive and prosper. We call these free-running former captives "feral" domesticates. They are not wild in the true (evolved) sense because they were created by artificial selection in domestication, but they have become untamed, and are living in the wild.

44

These feral domesticates always do best where the receiving area has already been disturbed by the human presence — most often by some degree of agriculture. After all, the animals have been selected to live in a human environment. Ingrates that they are, they require our "seed" subsidy in order to get started, but once on their own they turn on us — and, much more important, they turn on innocent bystanders. As saws and axes are extensions of the human arm, so feral domesticates are extensions of saws and axes. The way having been prepared for them by us, they proliferate at the expense of co-evolved indigenous communities which have already been traumatized and weakened by human alteration, homogenization, and simplification. The more specialized indigenous forms usually haven't a prayer because of the wide-spectrum feeding abilities of the exotics.

It is ironical that many of the features for which we bred these animals are those that make them most ecologically destructive in a feral state. Even in our wildest dreams we could not have hoped to succeed so dramatically in making them *just like us.*

It has been observed that only two kinds of animals — goats and people — actually create their own habitats. In the case of goats, the preferred habitat is desert.[16] There is a long and sad list of places in which natural vegetation and indigenous species dependent on it have been eliminated by goats. The best known example is the Galapagos archipelago.[17] The goats were first set loose by seventeenth-century seafarers in the apparent hope that the animals would serve as a continuing food supply for ships' personnel in the future. (Why they would do this is a mystery; in those days the islands abounded with slow-moving and easily obtainable land tortoises and iguanas, to say nothing of great tumultuous rookeries of seabirds and sea lions, and a cornucopia of delicious fishes.) There were subsequent goat releases onto islands not previously contaminated, some of them even in this century. As one who has tried to do his bit by eating a Galapagos goat, I can fully understand why the fresh meat supply has endured for so many years.

Goat devastation in the Galapagos is horrifying. Some islands are almost entirely denuded in places. But there is a great deal more that does not immediately meet the eye. There were no plant-eating mammals in the islands prior to the arrival of the goats. The browsers and grazers were all reptiles — giant land tortoises and large land iguanas. Slow and deliberate in their movements, they tended to eat what was right in front of them, and did not have either the metabolism or the agility to go searching for greener pastures when the goats removed their local food sources. Most of the races of both tortoises and land iguanas are now in dire peril on all their islands; some have vanished forever. There have been a number of goat-extermination campaigns mounted from time to time and from island to island, mostly with only moderate success.

The goats of Galapagos are not the familiar barnyard creatures. They are not the vaguely addled-looking beasts we are accustomed to seeing in confinement. These animals are alert, quick, and exceedingly shy. It is very difficult to approach them more closely than binocular range; having in mind the sharp, loose and tumbled broken lava that is the usual footing in Galapagos, it is no surprise that shooting sorties have been relatively unproductive. The steep terrain is made to order for goats, and they thrive on it. So extraordinarily adaptable are they that, if pressed, they can even drink sea water.

Goats are fast multipliers, and they have been here for more than three centuries. Not having been subject to artificial breeding selection for all that time, they have somehow (no one knows precisely how) not only "reverted" to keen alertness but also regained many of the other behavioural and physical attributes of the wild.[18] Many of the males are stunningly handsome, with massive curving horns and an all-round impressiveness of style and demeanour to go with them.[19] It is clear that they have shed many of the earmarks of domestication, perhaps most of them. But one, at least, remains. Their ecologic placelessness rings from the desertified hillsides, gleams from the whitened brittle carapaces of long-dead tortoises.

The Galapagos giant tortoises have been grievously affected by both feral domesticates and introduced rats. The rats attack little hatchlings before their shells have hardened sufficiently to protect them. Dogs also do this. Both dogs and pigs dig up and devour tortoise eggs from their underground nests. Donkeys trample and dust-bathe on top of the nests, making emergence difficult for the hatchlings. The tortoises, however, are only one of the aggrieved. Dogs commonly catch both land and marine iguanas, for example, and feral pigs devour just about whatever they come across.

But protecting the indigenous flora and fauna of Galapagos is not as easy as making a declaration of war against the intruders and then prosecuting it. Every action, it seems, begets new problems. A 1983 report is illustrative.

> *This is hardly a simple case of bad (recently arrived) guys vs. good (older resident) guys. For one thing, there are complex interrelationships among the exotic species themselves. The dogs, for instance, attack feral cattle and help keep cat populations in check. Any strategy aimed at totally wiping out feral dogs would have to take these kinds of facts into account.*
>
> *Other facts complicate any attempt at an overall battle plan for reducing exotic species. Goats, for example, were formerly selected as the prime target for eradication, until hunters realized that, in the absence of goats, vegetation quickly grew back, making it extremely difficult to spot the wild pigs slated for destruction.*[20]

No medication, it would seem, is without a side-effect of some kind. Since prevention is no longer an option in most parts of the world, one cannot but wonder whether the best remedy might be to let the feral disease run its course, guided by the hope that there will be something "natural" left to act as a nucleus for future repopulation. That, however, takes time. Evolutionary time.

Evolutionary time is not what the exotic invasion problem is all about. The infestation of all the continents and the oceanic islands by our transported "wrecking crew" has taken place in a ridiculously brief span of evolutionary time. Intercontinental sea travel, even at a modest level, likely began no earlier than the Egyptian era, probably at least 6,000 years after the agricultural revolution. What began very much earlier than that, however, was the intercontinental progress, on foot, of the exotic species *par excellence*, the domesticate of domesticates, Numero Uno.

There is no doubt about the identity of the first runaway exotic species, or about the role of that species in the extinction of other species worldwide. As ecologists Paul and Ann Ehrlich say, it seems "highly likely that humanity got an early start in the business of extinction."[21] The prehistoric evidence, circumstantial though it may be, is persuasive; in the historic period the evidence is no longer circumstantial. The extinction events of the last 100,000 years or so may well rival the four great kill-offs of the distant geological past.

There were, presumably, roughly as many species abroad in the world in the early Pleistocene two million years ago as there are today. But there was a difference. The Pleistocene produced an array of *very large* animals. Then, all at once, this "megafauna" was drastically reduced. The great creatures fell like dominos in an extinction spasm the like of which had not occurred, it would seem, since the obliteration of the dinosaurs. What made it dramatically different from other such events that had preceded it was the fact that species vanished *without replacement*. Extinction is a necessary half of the evolutionary process, as we

48

know. But the other half must always be the appearance of new forms to occupy new and presumably changing environments. That did not happen. The reasons are still being debated, but the most plausible theory yet advanced strongly implicates the human species. It is known as "Pleistocene overkill."[22]

The great mammalian extinction phase appears to have begun about 100,000 years ago, peaking in the neighbourhood of 30,000 years ago. Even those who oppose the human-overkill theory cannot deny that the megafauna extinctions coincided remarkably with the movements of *Homo* over and between the continents. It is no accident that the first human impact was felt in Africa (where an impoverished but recognizable Pleistocene megafauna does what it can to persist in the present day). It has been shown that about 30 percent of large mammal *genera* (not species) in Africa were rendered extinct from about 175,000 to 40,000 years ago.[23] Thirty percent extinction, comparatively speaking, is *low*. Other continents suffered much more heavily. Presumably some measure of ecological "equilibrium" had been struck between the large savannah species in Africa and the human predator over hundreds of thousands of years. The relationship was gradually tipped in favour of our developing hunting technology.

Things went rather more rapidly elsewhere, especially in North America. In only the last 30,000 years (roughly coincident with the human arrival), more than 100 species became extinct. The destruction is said to have peaked between 14,000 and 8,000 years ago. It represented a qualitative change in the structure of the natural community. The trend was similar in Britain and Europe, in the Middle East, and in Australia, again with a common date of about 30,000 years ago. The Asian record is less clear. It is possible that some of the Pleistocene giants lasted longer in what is now Siberia than they did elsewhere.

True, the Pleistocene was a period of wild and relatively sudden climatic change. Some of the very largest elephants, rhinos, ground sloths, bison, and others may not have been flexible enough to tolerate the rapid oscillations in temperature and thus in habitats, and the large herbivores may have dragged large carnivores down with them. Also, some have suggested that, since the early Pleistocene saw the emergence of very many new species, the events of the later part of the period were just an evening-up process. These may well have been contributing factors, but the common denominators throughout were the proliferation and dispersal of the human domesticate, and the remarkable coincidence of the timing of the exotic arrival in the several regions.

More recent events do nothing to challenge the overkill hypothesis, but tend to confirm it. The exotic primate arrived in Madagascar between 1,500 and 1,800 years ago, and forthwith did in six of the seven species of gigantic flightless elephant birds. Europeans polished off the last one in 1650. (The largest of these relics of Pleistocene giantism stood ten feet tall and may have weighed 1,000 pounds. The liquid contents of its egg have been estimated at over two gallons. These birds may have given rise to the legend of Sindbad and the roc.) While they were at it, early settlers in Madagascar also exterminated sixteen species of large terrestrial lemurs (none survives), an indigenous hog, and two sorts of small hippos, among others. Several of the remaining tree lemurs are teetering on the brink today.

When the Polynesian Maoris invaded New Zealand about 1,000 years ago, they found only three species of mammals but an amazing variety of large birds doing the things that mammals usually do —browsing and grazing. Nearly a third of these are gone today, including all twenty-seven species of large flightless moas, all of which were gone before Europeans arrived, and one of which rivalled the Madagascar elephant birds in stature. Subsequently white New Zealanders have introduced an appalling roster of mammalian browsers and grazers, with the results we have observed earlier in this chapter.

Although the Pleistocene overkill theory is still not accepted everywhere in academic circles, it really does not matter whether it is accepted or not. What does matter is the sum of the human accomplishment within *historic* time. It has been estimated that between 1600 and 1900 we eliminated about seventy-five birds and mammals (there is no count of other taxa), and between 1900 and the present another seventy-five (again species other than birds and mammals not being monitored). The British ecologist and resource manager Norman Myers remarks: "The rate from the year 1600 to 1900, roughly one species every 4 years, and the rate during most of the present century, about one species per year, are to be compared with a rate of possibly one per 1000 years during the 'great dying' of the dinosaurs."[24]

Many authorities feel that by the time we entered the decade of the 1980s we were already disposing of species (of all kinds) at the rate of one per day, and the number for the 1990s could well be one per hour.[25] No longer, of course, are we concentrating on "megafauna"; we have worked our way well down the scale of size. We have reduced, simplified, homogenized, and pauperized Nature everywhere on the planet to an extent that cannot be biologically recoverable. Extinct species never rise again; new species require untrammelled heterogeneity and purity of habitat. Neither would appear to be in the cards. The human achievement has been breathtaking in its suddenness, total in its scope. This could only be the work of a placeless being — in an ecological sense, one utterly lacking in both intrinsic inhibitions and extrinsic controls. Any feral domesticate starts with those basic attributes; only a technical primate could have pulled it off. There was no immune system on Earth to repel the exotic invader. Everywhere, the transplant "took."

THE
EXOTIC
IDEOLOGY

As the rogue primate overran the world in late Pleistocene and early recent times, not all of the accompanying baggage was hardware. There were tools and weapons, to be sure, both of which improved to such an extent over time that the Pleistocene megafauna was helpless before them. Destructive as the new hardware was, however, the new software — the accumulating *knowledge of how-to-do-it* — was downright devastating. Storable, retrievable, transmissible technique made the conquest possible, on any "natural" time scale, virtually overnight. Technology, as an aspect of culturing, changed much more rapidly than the methods of avoidance used by prey species. It was no contest.

After the peak exterminations between 30,000 years ago and the most recent withdrawal of the ice, and after world human colonization was roughly complete about 1,000 years ago, the non-human world entered a period of relative calm. Humans having established their beach-heads (initially at considerable cost to the most vulnerable indigenous forms), their impact may have lessened — temporarily. After the initial painful adjustments to the human presence, at least some elements of Nature, especially in extreme latitudes, appear to have been able to cope, for a while. This post-Pleistocene Camelot lasted about 500 years.

By this time, the radiation of human populations into a variety of environments meant that cultural prostheses were now evolving independently of one another. Like Darwin's Galapagos finches on the scattered and isolated islands of their archipelago, human societies had developed distinct differences. Cultural separateness, like reproductive isolation, produced new concepts. Descended as they were from a common ancestor, the various human populations ("ecotypes")[1] retained their biological inheritance in common, including their domesticated dependence on how-to-do-it, but the particular *content* of their ideologies (including how to apprehend the nature of reality) became profoundly different from society to society.[2]

Some of the world's people remained gatherer–hunters. The words are placed in that sequence because in such societies, always, gathering was by far the more important activity. Even though many people enjoyed a substantial intake of animal protein, it was probably in the form of gathered eggs, nestlings, larvae and other insect forms, small reptiles and amphibians, and newborn or crippled mammals. Hunting would be predominant only in the long winters of high latitudes. Those people who continued to gather and hunt into contemporary times, by the way, did not do so because of any inadequacy, incompetence, or incompleteness, the chauvinism of our own society notwithstanding. Such people are integrated with their environments. Gatherers and hunters are community co-participants.

Other human societies relied heavily on fishing — at their population levels, with no more negative effect than that of the gatherer–hunters. Others elected farming at various scales of intensiveness; still others chose animal herding. Such choices were no doubt determined as much by environment as by culture. They were probably rationalized ideologically only long after the fact. Both agriculture and pastoralism have been dire news for Nature.[3] Both have been the scourge of ground cover, topsoil, and watersheds; both have simplified, homogenized, and monoculturalized vast areas of the planet; both have displaced and destroyed whole populations, communities, and biotas; both have relentlessly advanced the insatiable appetites of the exotic wrecking crew of feral domesticates and their rogue primate masters.

Nevertheless, until the European Renaissance the effects of agriculture, pastoralism, and the domesticated wrecking crew had been mostly confined to their regions of origin. Subsistence agriculture appears to have arisen independently in several parts of the world, but its most massive effects were Eurasian and Mediterranean. Then, with the advent of sixteenth-century navigational techniques, came the era of the intercontinental warlords. As I have suggested, up until this time some human races had achieved at least a modest equilibrium with what remained of the prehuman natural communities of the world. The intercontinentalists changed everything forever. If indeed there had been a human/Nature Camelot, it was now officially over.

Earlier, the word "invasion" was used to characterize the penetration of a natural community by an exotic species. The Dutch elm fungus disease was distributed in North America by European elm bark beetles (stowed away in shipments of logs with the bark intact). The cattle egret[4] immigrated to South and North America from Africa apparently under its own steam. In the case of the prehistoric human proliferation over and between the continents we might rather be inclined to use the term "dispersal" to describe the gradual, natural spreading of species into new geographic areas. Whether the human dispersal was "natural" may be debatable, but let us for a moment assume that it was. It would certainly have been natural for both pastoralists and gatherer–hunters to move around, especially as they exhausted local food sources. As hunting techniques developed, no doubt people began to move seasonally, and to accompany migratory prey species such as wildebeest and caribou. It might even be seen as natural for the Pleistocene megafauna to collapse from our attentions in such catastrophic fashion, although the suddenness of the collapse suggests otherwise. But when human beings attacked and subjugated groups of other human beings, we should drop the word "dispersal." This is invasion in the purest sense.

Human attacks on other humans frequently (perhaps invariably) involve the phenomenon which has been termed "pseudospeciation,"[5] the use of violence toward one's own species of a sort which would normally be reserved for use against other species, such as prey animals. (This very occasionally happens among wild predatory animals, in which case it is seen as pathological.) Like the wild predator, we take the lives of other species as a matter of course. We are used to knocking meat animals over the head, and we do it with aplomb, because the two of us are of different species; when we decide to knock another human over the head, that human is no longer a person. As Joseph Meeker, author of *The Comedy of Survival*, has pointed out, "in the history of human culture... this remarkable behavior has become institutionalized."[6] When we can see another human as not being of our species, then it is a very short step to perceiving another social class, or another culture, or another human race, as another species, in which case the usual intraspecific modes of behaviour are suspended, and interspecific modes may kick in. The device is most often used on a grand scale in time of war, when the enemy is portrayed as non- or subhuman so that the necessary atrocities may be committed without inhibition. It is also useful within totalitarian societies or any others in the categorization of groups toward whom aggression may be contemplated.

Pseudospeciation has always sustained the practice of human slavery, just as speciesism has always justified animal slavery. It was rife in classical times, and later on it allowed the Spanish conquistadores to see the Aztecs and the Incas as a class of beings separate from and beneath white Europeans. The device appears to have been in widespread use throughout the age of intercontinental conquest and colonial imperialism, and continues, only faintly disguised, in the age of multinational mercantile imperialism. The invaders see themselves as qualitatively different from the invaded indigenous peoples, and behave accordingly.

The white invaders distributed through the world not only their exotic diseases and their exotic domesticated animals, but also their home-grown orthodoxies and heresies and other dogmas. They distributed gimmicks and gizmos and gadgets and techniques and technologies and the ideologies appropriate to sustain them. They brought the undiluted contents of their particular cultural prosthesis, and they broadcast them both by persuasion and by force.

It seems not unreasonable to wonder whether an ideology introduced into a foreign (immunity-deficient) human culture might have an effect similar to that of a measles bug, or a goat, or a mongoose, or a sailor on first glimpsing one of Madagascar's extraordinary terrestrial lemurs. Let us call the phenomenon the environmental impact of exotic ideologies.[7]

The active ingredient here is the *exoticness* of the introduced ideology, not the fact of the ideology. All human groups, societies, and cultures are sustained by ideologies. All human beings are the domesticated creatures of how-to-do-it, and all lean on their fabricated prosthetic devices. The human animal may not be "the" culturing animal, but it most certainly is the ideologizing animal.

By "ideology" I mean a structure of ideas generally shared across a culture or a society. It is composed of interlaced and interacting supporting beliefs, most of which are in the form of inherited, often unarticulated shared perceptions. Members of a particular society tend to receive and apprehend the nature of reality through the mediation provided by the prevailing ideology. As societies have members, ideologies have adherents. Before the days of intercontinental homogenization and simplification, human societies the world over had developed ideologies appropriate to their environmental circumstances. Their ideologies grew out of those circumstances. They were indigenous.

Such peoples, domesticated primates though they were, had reached a reasonable *rapprochement* with their immediate surroundings. Unquestionably the most important factors here were the levels of their populations and technologies. Nature was still keeping the lid on. There were simply too few people, with too limited techniques, for them to do grievous damage. Their exoticness was gradually diluted and diminished (or at least masked or camouflaged) after settlement. But their domesticity remained. Nowhere may the human presence be seen as fully integrated and "natural," because wherever we may be, or however long we may have been there, we are still domesticates. Domesticates have no ecologic place, and they show it consistently and universally. When non-European indigenous peoples received and began to use firearms, for example, they revealed their exotic placelessness without missing a beat.

The exotic ideology rests upon a dualistic image of the relationship between human beings and all other natural phenomena. Its stance is human chauvinist; its program is Baconian conquest; its means is Cartesian rationality; its instruments are science and technology. It is human imperialism in its most highly developed form. Originally a localized northern aberration, it is now world-dominant.

Beginning in the sixteenth century, the export of the exotic ideology tended to be from Europe outward and southward, from
temperate latitudes to subtropical and tropical ones. The penetration of high latitudes took a little longer. It is interesting that our
domesticated animals, like the navigators, sprang from the
Mediterranean countries.[8] (It took a long time for us to manufacture cattle that could endure certain tropical conditions.) Our Western
(northern) prosthetic device, complete with its exotic ideology, is
of Mediterranean zone origin as well. As the tame homing pigeon
flies, it is a hop of only a few hundred miles from western Syria,
hotbed of ungulate domestication, to Hellas, seedbed of northern
ideology. At one time (pre-domestic goat), both were verdant.

I have described an ideology as a structure of interacting component beliefs. All ideologies develop through a process of mul-
tidimensional mutualistic interaction and relationships. Just as
lion and zebra and giraffe and hyena evolved together as an interdependent group, so too our European science, philosophy, technology, and assorted belief systems evolved over time. Our ideology
evolved as a unit. It is no accident that our science fits our philosophy fits our technology fits the convoluted belief system that
sustains them. Like the African savannah wildlife community,
they go together, and they are appropriate, each to all the others,
in a mutually supporting community of common interest.

The total interwoven package we no longer call European.
Until very recently we called it Western, or Euro-American, but
now we call it northern. Except for its selectively changing usage
in geopolitical rhetoric, the modifier has little importance. What
does matter is the self-righteous zeal with which the package is
advanced. Within it are varying measures of the several mutually sustaining ideologies of scientism, determinism, historicism,
fundamentalist evangelism, and the free-wheeling technological
chauvinism of the industrial growth imperative. It is important

58

to note here that the exotic ideology transcends political persuasion. Both "right" and "left" subscribe to and are subsumed by the greater ideology of the industrial-growth ethos.

The product and its promotion are administered by the multinational technocratic élite. No rationalization or justification of the product is required; the virtues of the ideology, like those of other manifest truths, are self-evident. The contemporary codeword for the advancement of the industrial enterprise through the consumption of Nature is "development."[9]

This process is often viewed in retrospect as an exercise in the domination of (a) human societies, or (b) Nature, or both. I doubt that there was at any time a conscious articulated *intent* to dominate anyone or anything. If we must see "domination," then we should see it as a means, not an end. Indigenous peoples provided handy slave labour, and that was convenient, but the goal was wealth, not human subjugation.[10] If Native peoples had to be destroyed toward the advancement of the greater purpose, that would be seen as regrettable, but also as necessary — an unavoidable peripheral "incalculable" or "externality." If they were not utilizable, Native peoples were simply in the way. The humanization of the planet means the face-lifting of the planet in *our* image, not some other image. Pseudospeciation helps here. The conquest is not of people. The conquest is of animate and inanimate "resources."[11]

The exotic ideology has been advanced in the last few decades under a variety of banners. The words may change, but the message is constant. "Resource management," of course, is now a centenarian; of more recent arrival was "resource development." This soon mutated into the lunatic term "ecodevelopment," one which, despite some very considerable expenditure of effort, I was never able to penetrate. At roughly the same time we had "appropriate technology," which was perilously close to being internally contradictory. At the present moment we have "sustainable development," a full-blown oxymoron. What these slogans seem to say is "How to plunder Nature and get away with it." A cultural and ideological imperative, which only a domesticate deprived of ecologic sensibility could have conceived in the first place.

Development is a fascinating concept. In the sense in which I learned to understand it, development means the gradual unfolding or realization of an organism, a community — or even an idea — toward a richer, finer, fuller, higher, or more mature state of being. The metamorphosis of a Luna moth, the emergence of a new seral stage in meadow succession, the growth of an embryo, the flowering of a thesis. In the contemporary technoculture, the word "development" is used to describe land speculation, land subdivision, construction, and the work of the wrecker's ball on cherished old buildings in the city core. "Development" is also used to describe the advancement of the exotic ideology. It represents the crushing and scarification of forests, the mutilation and corruption of waterways, the savaging and toxification of the living soils.

The "development" ideologues do not hear the screaming of the buttressed trees or the wailing of the rivers or the weeping of the soils. They do not hear the sentient agony and the anguish of the non-human multitudes — torn, shredded, crushed, incinerated, choked, dispossessed.[12] These are merely the external, incalculable, and incidental side-effects of the necessary progress of human civilization in its highest form.

"Development," in its current usage, stands for the advancement of the exotic ideology and the subjugation of those *external* phenomena we call Nature. All of this, if only by definition, means bringing that which is not human (together with non-industrialized humans, obviously) toward a richer, finer, fuller, higher, more mature state of being. And, given the progressive, deterministic bias of the exotic ideology, this process is preordained and *necessary*.

The German critic Wolfgang Sachs has observed that "he who

pronounces the word [development] denotes nothing, but claims the best of intentions. Development... has no content, but it does possess a function: it allows any intervention to be sanctified in the name of a higher, evolutionary goal."[13]

"Development" thus insists that the (industrial) human state of being is an evolutionary achievement over, above, and beyond other states of being, and that the purpose and destiny of Earth and its non-human occupants is to be remade in the human image.[14] As Sachs puts it, "through the trick of a biological metaphor, a simple economic activity turns into a natural and evolutionary process, as though hidden qualities would be progressively developed to their final state. The metaphor thus says that the real destiny of natural goods is to be found in their economic utilization; all economic uses are a step forward to direct inner potential toward that goal."[15] The process must be sustained. That is what the ideology of industrial growth is all about.

The element of *growth* must be stressed. Industrialization by itself is insufficient. Although we often hear calls for a "stable" economy, what is meant is an economy that does not stop growing. An economy that is stable is a dead economy. The industrial-growth economy, in its insatiability for raw materials and markets, has done whatever it needed to do in order to obtain them. Colonial imperialism plundered the non-temperate world for raw materials; modern multinational imperialism, while continuing that tradition, is simultaneously engaged in the creation of mass-consumption markets in its own image. The record shows abundantly and vividly that the industrial "system" will do whatever is necessary to achieve its ends: when politicking, wheedling, and cajoling are insufficient, it has no inhibitions against violence. In the latter case, recourse to pseudospeciation, once again, is useful.

"Development" has become an international project dedicated to the advancement of the industrial-technological ideology. Let us attempt to separate out some of the ingredients of which it is made. In his *Arrogance of Humanism* David Ehrenfeld uses the term "end-product analysis" to describe "the necessarily informal study of effects that sum up many causes."[16] I have asserted that the industrial/technological ideology is "exotic" (meaning placeless) quite simply on the overwhelming body of evidence of its destructiveness the world over. That is the end product. I have asserted that it is chauvinistic on the grounds that the industrial/technological state of being is taken as a "development" over other states of being. What is important here is that the "developed" condition is seen as not only necessary but also inevitable. Popular catch-words of the day are illustrative: "pre-industrial," "underdeveloped," or "developing" societies. The patronizing paternalism inherent in such language I shall not dwell on here; for our purposes the operative element is the implication of historical *necessity*.

"Historicism" is a term used by the philosopher Karl Popper to describe, for example, Marx's notion that scientific laws underlie the development of history: "I mean by 'historicism' an approach to the social sciences which assumes that *historical prediction* is their principal aim, and which assumes that this aim is attainable by discovering the 'rhythms' or the 'patterns', the 'laws' or the 'trends' that underlie the evolution of history."[17]

Bryan Magee elaborates:

Examples of historicist beliefs are: that of the Old Testament Jews in the mission of the Chosen People; that of the early Christians in the inevitability of mass conversions to be followed by the Second Coming; that of some Romans in the destiny of Rome to rule the world; that of Enlightenment liberals in the inevitability of progress and the perfectibility of man; of so many Socialists in the inevitability of Socialism; that of Hitler in the establishment of a Thousand

62

*Year Reich. One has only to start listing some of the more
famous examples to note their low fruition-rate. But apart
from specific theories, the general notion that history must
have a destination, or if not that a plot, or at any rate a
meaning, or at least some sort of coherent pattern, seems
to be widespread.*[18]

To Magee's examples one could add: (a) the preferred humanist interpretation of the palaeontological record of organic evolution (the destination: us); (b) the preferred industrial/mercantile
interpretation of the history of intercontinental expansionism (the
destination: worldwide "development"); and (c) the preferred
"civilized" interpretation of the history of science and technology (the destination: one predictable and controllable world). In
those three contexts, the fuel of historicism is the deeper humanistic need for unequivocally anthropocentric purpose and meaning in the universe.

Historicist interpretations of human evolution, of the record
of intercontinentalist accretions, and of science and technology
readily produce the conclusion of human special privilege on Earth,
the truth of which is manifest. That such phenomena constitute
"progress" is also obvious and unchallengeable. To contest them
would be irrational.

The exotic ideology as advanced by the international "development" technocracy is fundamentally dependent for its authen-
ticity and authority on scientific rationality and its many
appendages. The scientific mystique purveyed rests basically on
reduction and quantification, by means of which the prediction
and control of Nature are made possible. The reduction and quantification of Nature in turn require the objectification of Nature.
Most commonly, this is carried out by the branch of biological
science called ecology. As a science, ecology depends not only on
objective quantification but also on the mechanistic and econo-

mistic models it has drawn from both the physical and the social sciences.[19]

Ecology, like any other science, proceeds from a number of assumptions. As often as not, those assumptions are rooted in metaphoric expressions of "reality" which we use to explain the inexplicable. Too often, our metaphors are reified. We have out-grown the clockwork universe, but similar devices remain today to plague ecology and thus our understanding of what ecology has to say to us. Take, for example, the mechanistic and the economistic versions of natural "reality." They are, of course, interdependent and mutually reinforcing. The two are widely purveyed, both in contemporary technocratic planning and management and in the liberal humanist versions of modern "environmentalism." Both are fundamental supporting buttresses of the exotic ideology.

An aside: nothing in this analysis is to be taken as an attempt to represent any conscious collusion between elements of the problem that is being described. Every domesticate requires a prosthesis; in the case of the human domesticate, that prosthesis is the knowledge of how-to-do-it; ideology allows its adherents to receive, apprehend, and rationalize the world in terms of how-to-do-it. Various versions of this evolved in various parts of the world. One of them has proven disastrous not only in its region of origin, but also, through export, in areas foreign to it. No conspiracy is required. The technocratic élite and humanist society at large are true believers.

The historicist interpretation of all this is quite simple: on the basis of the visible record of the progressive expansion of the exotic ideology, clearly there was a destination built in, or if not that, a plot or a story-line, or at least a purpose and meaning, or at the very least a coherent pattern. This is where ecology comes in, to offer a properly scientific and thus hygienic rationale for what has happened.

Ecology is an undeniably useful and intensely interesting body of theory and knowledge. Some of its practitioners describe it as the study of the structure and function of Nature. This might strike one as somewhat broad, having in mind the total roster of both theoretical and applied physical, biological, and social sciences, all of which may reasonably be seen as addressing the structure and function of Nature. Julian Huxley, years ago, described ecology as "scientific natural history." This was probably the best definition at that time. More recently, ecology would seem to have become what I would call *scientistic* natural history. By this is meant the inescapable contemporary chauvinism of objective observation and quantification. Although many ecologists are still naturalists, many are not, preferring to remain in the comfortable abstract environment of rational piecemeal scientific measurement and prediction. Naturalists study whole living beings; scientists study data. There is often ill-disguised contempt for naturalists, who love unfragmented Nature on its own terms, which is to say non-rationally.

As a part of the prosthetic device (knowledge of how-to-do-it), ecology both informs and is informed by its sibling parts, all of which are perceptually (and metaphysically) governed by the filtering historicist ideology. Of radical importance to the symbiotic relationship between ideology and science is the unceasing interchange between the two. One example among many is the ecological maxim known as the "competitive exclusion principle," which is often translated as "competitors cannot co-exist."

This is surely not a biological principle but an economic one. Everybody knows that competition is the driving force of the free marketplace, and that competition is about somebody winning and somebody else losing. Everybody also knows that the very concept of competition requires in the competitor some form of goal-orientation. Although few if any naturalists would be able to perceive either winners or losers in Nature, and few would ascribe goal-orientation to non-human organisms, competition in Nature is inferred steadfastly and without question throughout the entire corpus of ecology. A standard expression of ecological competition: "Competition in the broadest sense refers to the interaction of two organisms striving for the same thing. Interspecific competition is any interaction that adversely affects the growth and survival of two or more species populations.... Simultaneously, competition triggers many selective adaptations that enhance the coexistence of a diversity of organisms in a given area or community."[20]

In a more recent publication, the same author (E.P. Odum, probably the most authoritative voice in modern ecology) puts it more succinctly: "The word competition denotes a striving for the same thing, as in the familiar case of two businesses striving for the same market."[21] There is absolutely no qualification or equivocation here. Competition is natural, and competition is good. The "competitive exclusion principle" is invoked to explain the undeniably apparent fact that "closely related organisms having similar habits or morphologies *often* do not occur in the same places. If they do occur in the same places, they *frequently* use different resources [*sic*] or are active at different times" (emphasis added).[22]

So the competitive exclusion rule does not always apply. And non-human organisms are resource exploiters,[23] just like us. The anthropomorphic language of ecology aside, the competitive marketplace model of natural process allows us to perceive Nature quite comfortably in terms of the exotic ideology — as a cut-and-thrust commercial rat-race geared to the survival of the most aggressive.

Central to the maintenance of this image of the "reality" of Nature and of natural process is the concept of "niche," defined succinctly as the "role, function, or place of [an] organism."[24] The niche of a species is not merely spatial; it is also described by what the species does — how it makes its living, how it fits into the larger community, how it affects other species.

66

There is something tautological about the concept of niche. This is because a niche exists only when it is occupied. We postulate a niche for every plant and animal we see in any community. If a given situation is apparently undisturbed and "natural," and a given type of organism is absent, then we conclude that there is no niche for it. Or is there? As Donald Worster, historian of ideas, says, "The niche is the species and the species is the niche."[25] We can infer an "open" niche if we know that some species has been locally exterminated, or we can readily perceive a new niche when a new species arrives. If it is there, ergo, it has found a niche. It has won the competition for a place.[26]

Yet, as we have seen, ecologically placeless ("nicheless") feral domesticated species have been extravagantly successful. We see the goat on its denuded Galapagos hillside; must we now infer that it has a niche after all? It is plain that the goat is there, and that it *does* things: it eats, and it defecates, and it reproduces, and it dies — all healthy and entirely proper for any animal. It even interacts with other species — negatively, to be sure, but it clearly has a "role" in the community, no matter how repellant that role may appear to us.

So, by extension, we might see the human domesticate, and so indeed the exotic ideology. They are *here*; ergo, they have niches. There is no gainsaying the fact that the rogue primate, and its feral artifacts, have been biologically successful.[27] They have *outcompeted* other species. Also, one human ideology among many has overcome other ideologies. That, ecology can say, is in the competitive nature of things.

This is a truly vexatious question. In the context of exotic introductions, whether rabbit or mongoose or goat or rogue primate, or indeed ideology, niche theory becomes exceedingly problematical. Such is the case because, when a transplant fails to "take," we infer the absence of a niche for it. When it does catch on, we infer a pre-existing niche. Yet few if any wildlife ecologists, one would think, would see any feral domesticate as "belonging" in the sense of contributory integration — of properly occupying either a spatial or a functional space in any natural community.

On the other hand, the ecologist who is competition-oriented *must* see it so. On marketplace analysis, which is what competition theory dictates, there is no alternative to that conclusion. But surely competition would not be a factor where the way has actually been *prepared* for the exotic domesticate. Non-human feral domesticates have a much better chance of "succeeding" if the way has been paved for them by some measure of prior human settlement. The more the local environment has been impoverished by human activity, the better the human satellites like it. This does not strike one as a "competitive" situation. It would follow that the white European human domesticate itself was in the same way the beneficiary where it found an established indigenous human presence. This would have provided a useful running start for the exploitation of local resources.

Through the long period of colonialism and intercontinental mercantilism, "original" peoples were allowed access only to those elements of European technology that were good for them, meaning good for the mercantile enterprise. All this remained relatively unchanged until after the Second World War. The onset of the postwar political independence movement began to bring the exotic ideology to its fullest international flowering.

Prior to that time, it had been necessary to convert or indoctrinate only a few tame local adjutants and other minor functionaries. The imperial invaders owned and operated their far-flung multicontinental establishments, and ran them as they saw fit by means of an introduced population of home-grown bureaucrats. Over this long period, the flags of Britain, France, Spain, Holland, Portugal, and so on were (often literally) interchangeable; this

made not the slightest difference to the process of European parasitism. More interesting is the fact that over those centuries of
colonialism the gradually evolving industrial-cum-technological
Euro-American ideology stayed largely at home; in the foreign
mercantile possessions it was chiefly restricted to the hearts and
minds of foreign-serving white satraps.

The postwar independence movement changed everything. As a
growing procession of former European colonies began to run up
their own flags, traditional northern greed and cupidity began to be
tempered by the first faint twinges of fear. Fear of both the depletion of God-given "resources" at home, and fear of the loss of cheap
materials from abroad. Fear also of change and possible slippage in
foreign markets. Gut fear being a sharper and more insistent moti-
vator than even old-fashioned avarice, things began to happen.

As Wolfgang Sachs explains it,[28] old-style colonialism was
motivated by both profit and the moral authority of Europeans
in their mission to raise the Natives to a higher state of being (the
latter task, thanks to Rudyard Kipling, has long been known as
the white man's burden). In the postwar period the two were con-
flated into the idea of development, the northern industrial and
economic order being seen as the highest form of civilization. The
U.S. mission to advance its ideological and commercial hegemony was vastly aided and abetted by the *symbolic* effect of its technology on the imaginations of "underdeveloped" nations. As Sachs
puts it, in the 1950s and 1960s, the new nations all tended to
adopt the same path, the same goal, and all began to lose touch
with their individual origins and their indigenous ways.

By the early 1970s, Sachs says, it had become evident that in
such countries the rich élites were becoming richer, the poor, poorer. This necessitated the extension of the *idea* of development to
include equity and social assistance. In the same fashion, the idea
of development has now been further extended to include the

healing of the environmental injuries it has caused. Each successive problem occasioned by development has been met by a further extension of its definition, to the point that the idea itself is now bereft of all meaning. Sachs feels that the current slogan "sustainable development" arises out of the need to rationalize the undeniable fact that commercial development means environmental disruption with the undiminishing desire to advance the politics of economic growth.

The most important export of the northern industrial-growth ideology has always been itself, meaning both its means and its ends. It is a commonplace that foreign aid has always carried a price consisting of required bloc alignments both political and economic. This is quite normal. Alliances of convenience have existed since there have been human states and communities of self-interest. Much more important is the fact that the true and non-refundable price of foreign aid today is whole and unreserved commitment to and service in multinational commerce. This in turn requires unconditional surrender and committed obeisance by the recipient nation to the exotic ideology.

The simplified, homogenized, monoculturalized industrial-growth imperative has become world-pervasive. "Developing" nations and peoples have become domesticated into the alien way, servants of an external agent of control in a process that they have been indoctrinated into believing is "natural" and "progressive." Such is the way of historicism. This is how it was *meant* to be.

A final irony in the industrial domestication of "emerging" nations is evident in the fact that the northern way of seeing and believing is advanced *by invitation*. Every people, every society must have its prosthetic ideology. Since the possessors of the old, indigenous versions were so readily overwhelmed by the colonial imperialists, clearly the latter had better ways of apprehending reality. The removal of the old, environmentally integrated perceptual lenses and their replacement with the new technocratic version is facilitated by the rise to power of foreign-trained political and bureaucratic élites.

Immersed in the exotic ideology, seeing the exotic ideology as wholly natural and appropriate, and indispensable in the modern world, these most sophisticated of all domesticates are only too anxious to embrace whatever cultural transplant is offered by their old northern chums from MBA school. In the process of neutralizing any vestiges of a cultural immune system from within, they import more experts, more consultants, more technicians, more resource administrators, more "environmental" planners, more micro-computer salesmen, more priests of the exotic ethos of "sustainable development." Like goats and rabbits, such transplants "take."

Such is the nature of world conquest by a system of ideas and beliefs indigenous originally to Europe, exotic everywhere else. It rests fundamentally on Western philosophy, science, and technology, together constituting a metaphysics peculiar to its area of origin. It is anointed and sanctified through the manifest truth of its extraordinary success in competition with ideologies indigenous to other parts of the world. Its advancement is understood to be necessary and inevitable. It purveys the image of a mechanistic, economistic, rationalistic, humanistic universe. It says nothing about Nature.

NATURE'S MARKETPLACE

The competitive, mercantile interpretation of the world legitimates and justifies the exotic industrial ideology as proper, progressive, and "natural." It has for many years also informed most branches of the formal study of animal behaviour. Within individual species the most intensive focus of the economistic bias has been on social and spatial organization. The unseen hand of striving, self-serving competition has been accepted as the "given" underlying principle in such constructions as social-dominance hierarchy and territoriality. The major root-stalk from which sprang the bourgeois marketplace bias of both generalized and behavioural ecology is to be found in the nineteenth-century interpretation of Darwinian evolutionary theory.

Even now there remains the widespread belief that Charles Darwin "discovered" or "invented" evolution. He did neither. His immortal contribution was a theory of *how evolution works*:

by natural selection.[1] Many of his peers and antecedents (including his own grandfather) had already accepted the fact of evolution having occurred, but no one had come up with a defensible notion of what had actually happened. Darwin offered just that, and changed forever the way in which human beings perceive the organic world. (It took a while for the intellectual "paradigm" to accept the unbroken, continuing, and ongoing nature of selection, most especially with regard to our own species.)

Science, like animal husbandry, practises artificial selection. It chooses which strains shall be perpetuated and further developed, which shall be discarded. In this way, new scientific realities, like new breeds of fancy pigeons, may be brought on stream with, relatively speaking, blinding rapidity. As it happened (it could not have been otherwise), Darwin selected elements of the social and natural science of his day in mounting and defending his thesis.[2] Among many others, we find legacies of Hobbes (nasty and brutish combat in Nature), Adam Smith (free and universal competition), Locke (the primacy of the individual), Malthus (the limits to subsistence), de Candolle (a perpetual state of "war" in Nature), and Lyell (the struggle for existence).

No scientist or any other thinker is immune to the accepted ideas of a time. "Like every other scientist, Darwin approached nature, human nature, and society with ideas derived from his culture."[3] His ideas, and those of his contemporary (and competitor?) Alfred Russel Wallace "reflected the belief widespread among their countrymen in progressive improvement through individual, national, and racial competition."[4] No doubt this is why Thomas Huxley saw Darwin's theory as a blinding flash of the obvious. It was, after all, imperial Britain of the middle of the nineteenth century. Darwin offered an image of the organic world wholly in keeping with the dominant ideological prosthesis of his day.

Since the social thought of our own time is at some variance with that of the 1850s, one might wonder how it is that so much of Darwin's argument remains today in relatively unchanged form. It would seem that although nice people no longer entertain (or at least publicly express) notions such as Malthus's social apocalypticism or Darwin's own élitism and implicit (even explicit) racism, Victorian competitive economistic ideology continues to flourish in scientific thought. Only the grossest social implications of Darwinism have been selected out; its fundamental scientific paradigm remains unimpaired.

Darwin was firm on the matter of competition. The third chapter of the *Origin* is titled "Struggle for Existence." Early in that chapter, Darwin sets the ground rules.

> *The elder De Candolle and Lyell have largely and philosophically shown that all organic beings are exposed to severe competition.... Nothing is easier than to admit in words the truth of the universal struggle for life, or more difficult — at least I have found it so — than constantly to bear this conclusion in mind. Yet unless it be thoroughly engrained in the mind, I am convinced that the whole economy of nature, with every fact on distribution, rarity, abundance, extinction, and variation, will be dimly seen or quite misunderstood.[5]*

In other words, either the reader accepts that Nature is an "economy" characterized by universal competitive struggle, or the ensuing 428 pages will convey little or nothing. We have been warned, categorically.

And, make no mistake, evolutionary process by competitive natural selection is to be seen as *progressive*. This fitted well with Victorian social norms, and with the emerging ethos of the industrial-growth society. There are repeated references to progress, improvement, and winning and losing in the "race for life."[6]

Darwin illustrates this by way of domesticated breeds of animals, showing how new breeds replace "older and inferior kinds."[7] Newer is better — a strikingly contemporary thought.

Implications of progress, improvement, and victory rising out of competition were to have great importance in due course, when the humanists were going to have to swallow the fact of organic evolution, and of human involvement in it. The human species (especially, it must be said, in its northern European form) was the ultimate victor, the heroic end-product of the titanic struggles of the past. One is led to wonder whether, without this nakedly chauvinistic dimension, Darwin's thesis might have taken somewhat longer than it did to enter mainstream Western thought. We should not, however, suspect Darwin of providing icing sugar for the establishment. He was a true Anglican believer, to be sure, but he was also fully persuaded of the integrity of his evidence and his argument, which is best encapsulated thus:

> ... the more recent forms must, on my theory, be higher than the more ancient; for each new species formed by having had some advantage in the struggle for life over other and preceding forms.... I do not doubt that this process of improvement has affected in a marked and sensible manner the organisation of the more recent and victorious forms of life, in comparison with the ancient and beaten forms...[8]

As though to wrap up the interplay of Victorian imperial ideology and social theory with emerging evolutionary biology, in his concluding recapitulation Darwin comments as follows on the matter of exotic transplants:

> As natural selection acts by competition, it adapts the inhabitants of each country only in relation to the degree of perfection of their associates; so that we need feel no surprise

at the inhabitants of any one country, although on the ordi-
nary view supposed to have been specially created and adapt-
ed for that country, being beaten and supplanted by the
naturalised production from another land.[9]

The implication is clear. Because of the varying quality of com-
peting forms, evolutionary emergences in one place may be less
perfect than those in another place. Competition in the bush
leagues is not as demanding as competition in the major leagues.
"In 1881, less than a year before his death, [Darwin] expressed
to William Graham his conviction that the Caucasian race had
'beaten the Turkish hollow in the struggle for existence' and predicted that the 'lower races' would soon be eliminated by the
'higher civilized races' throughout the world."[10]

In Victorian England this was not an unusual thought. It is
included here not to attempt to tarnish Darwin's achievement,
but rather to again underscore the intimate symbiotic relationships between the various elements that comprise any ideology.
Here, the common thread is the presumed universality of progress
necessarily arising from superiority in a competitive struggle.
Competition is "natural," and good, and winning is even better.

Assuming, as I do, that Darwin did not raise the competitive
struggle in Nature merely as a "selling" device for his theory, but
because he was fully persuaded of it himself, one can only wonder
how someone so monumentally gifted as both an observer and a
theorist could hew so firmly to an ideology so fundamentally anthropomorphic and so contradictory to the states of being every naturalist encounters every day. On the thesis presented in this book,
Darwin as an individual may be seen as the domesticated artifact
of the cultural ideology of his day. He felt obliged, intellectually, to
make his case as strongly as possible within the accepted rules. What
he had to say was so revolutionary that he naturally packaged it as
firmly as possible within the prevailing academic wisdom. We need

not think that he made a conscious choice in this respect; he did exactly what his own world-view dictated that he do.

Darwin was a complex man. He had pangs of conscience, albeit briefly, over the theological implications of his work. And in spite of the rigour of his formal analysis, he shows much of the unself-conscious joy of Nature appreciation traditional in British natural history. He was the greatest naturalist of his day, perhaps of all time, and he deeply loved Nature. There are moving passages in the *Origin*, places in which Darwin reveals motivations and feelings that lie very close to the cool scientific surface. The final paragraph, after summarizing natural selection and the struggle for existence, concludes: "There is grandeur in this view of life, with its several powers, having been originally breathed into a few forms or into one; and that, whilst this planet has gone cycling on according to the fixed law of gravity, from so simple a beginning endless forms most beautiful and most wonderful have been, and are being, evolved."[11]

This is a statement of wonder, and of awe. In it, and in numerous other places throughout his work, Darwin reveals a spiritual connection to Nature which has been largely masked and obscured by his scientific contribution. Science picked up competitive struggle and ran with it; the "soul" of Charles Darwin has been mostly forgotten.

Nowhere has competition been more widely and flagrantly invoked as the fount of all individual interaction than in studies of intraspecies (especially intragroup) non-human social behaviour. Competition explains virtually all actions and reactions within the social order. Competition itself, however, need not be explained. It is a self-evident, manifest truth. Especially pernicious has been the widespread attribution of competitive striving for dominance to individuals of highly social species, from chickens to chimpanzees.

"All social animals are 'status-seekers.'"[12] Although this, from Konrad Lorenz, is perhaps the bluntest assertion yet made on the subject, it is a reasonable encapsulation of the conventional wisdom. If it is reminiscent of the "inferiority complex" and the concomitant "drive" for superiority and the "will to power" that were part of the conventional wisdom of the early years of this century, that is probably no accident. The concept of the "pecking order"[13] emerged in the 1920s to a receptive scientific audience, entered the popular idiom, and has found a firm, fast, and as yet ineradicable place in our shared cultural perspective of Nature.

The pecking order was originally about barnyard chickens. It was observed that individual birds within a flock will establish an order of precedence in feeding, and that the sequence from first to last (a "linear hierarchy") is fairly stable and unchanging. It was also observed that the first or "top" bird, usually called Alpha, will peck or threaten to peck another who attempts to usurp her place (meaning: who attempts to feed). The intruder almost always will back off. This is generally described as "deference." Everyone defers to Alpha.

It was also observed that, if you remove the reigning Alpha, her place will be taken immediately by another bird, the new Alpha. This is too easily construed — both popularly and scientifically — as evidence that the second bird was all the while awaiting the opportunity for an advancement in her status. If you keep removing the temporary Alphas you will find that all of the birds are hungry, because all of them eventually approach the food. This can easily be taken as in-built, innate chicken acquiescence to authority. The reasonable possibility that the individual chicken may not feel either dominant or submissive — that it may feel quite comfortable and secure in its social arrangements — is not usually entertained. Status may not mean anything to a chicken.

Chicken fanciers know that it is not a good idea to unsettle a flock by continually removing birds and replacing them with new ones, because social relationships do not have time to sort themselves out, and the birds are put off their feed. Familiarity confers stability to the order of precedence, and all individuals are the better for it.

Chicken fanciers also know that it is not a good idea to put all of the birds' food in one heap, or container, or all of their water in one dish. They know that any pecking-order experiments are begging to be rigged. The objective observer of striving for dominance, in order to elicit the pecking order, must *stress* the hungry or thirsty birds by putting all the food or drink in one bowl. (It would help also to deprive them of both in anticipation of the experiment.) If the food were scattered about the whole henyard, and if water were made available in two or three places, no hierarchical experimental results would ensue. Status seeking would not be evident.

It seems clear that such experiments simulate an acute food or water shortage, thereby placing the birds under unaccustomed strain. A similar effect can be achieved by crowding them. It would appear that, in a wild state, the birds are genetically predisposed to respond to distress in certain ways. In periods of difficulty — drought, famine, severe overpopulation — it would be desirable that at least some individuals survive long enough to act as a breeding nucleus for better times. These would likely be the strongest individuals, to whom others might very well "defer" as in the barnyard experiments. Such an apprehension of chicken (or wild jungle fowl) social behaviour and organization does not require the attribution of a will to power, a drive to dominate, or competitive status seeking. Nor does it even illustrate competition for scarce food — not if some individuals "defer" to others.

In any severe situation, it is among the rank and file of a social group that the effects will be apparent first. Poor diet could reduce the survival of young, lower disease resistance, or make certain individuals more vulnerable to predation, or impair their reproductive cycles. In evolutionary terms, these would be selected *out*.

The stronger, healthier survivors would be selected *in*, to reproduce and pass along whatever qualities enabled them to endure the crisis. If one wishes to put it that way, a (pre-Darwinian) "struggle for existence" could be inferred, but it would require a lively imagination to see it as a competitive one, and rare creativity to see it as the result of intragroup social striving for dominance.

Chickens can be combative, and they can be induced to demonstrate their combativeness very easily. The essence of the cock fight is to subject the animals to distress. Chicken social niceties being what they are, it is unusual for two prime roosters to encounter each other at close quarters. When they do, it is the usual convention for them to avoid each other, to "defer" to each other's presence and thus to improve the odds against an encounter. If they are forced closely together, they will fight. They *must* fight, because chicken social mores dictate plenty of space between breeding cocks.

The cock fight is stage-managed by confining two male birds in an arena so small that they have no means of mutual avoidance. There is only one thing for them to do, and they do it. Neither is aggressively[14] attempting to dominate the other, neither is fighting for status or Alpha position, but both are fighting for their lives. I have heard it said that it is the denial of "escape distance" that triggers the fight; in ordinary circumstances there would be room for the weaker cock to give way before the stronger. I think it is more likely that there is not sufficient space for two *personal distances*, the personal distance of a mature cock bird being very different from that of a hen.

The language conventionally used to describe animal behaviour reveals a great deal about human attitudes. The term "pecking order" clearly connotes fierceness and aggressiveness. It implies that there is a hierarchical order of dominance in the henyard, maintained by overt physical violence. This, as we have seen, is patently untrue. As it happens, the term has mostly disappeared from the scientific vocabulary. Unfortunately, it lives and thrives in popular language, and serves as a radical support for the preferred cultural image of Nature as an arena for bloody, cut-throat competition for personal status.

Still very robust in the scientific literature, however, are words such as "aggression," "competition," "dominance" and "submission," "hierarchy," and, of course, "territoriality."[15] What matters is not the words, but the taint of Victorian chauvinism they convey. Most scientists would decry Lorenz's bald statement on universal status seeking as ludicrous, but the sense of his assertion is confirmed in terms used every day in the study of non-human social behaviour. All of the above imply (indeed require) overt struggle for individual status within a group power structure.

Paradoxically, most scientists (and humanists in general) have always been loath to permit the attribution to non-human individuals of the capacity for self-awareness. One would think that an urge for individual status-achievement could arise only from the desire to satisfy an awareness of self-interest. Why "compete" otherwise? And even if a competitive drive were built in, when the individual achieved a certain status, how would it know, in the absence of self-identity, that it had "arrived"? Surely striving for dominance requires self-awareness.[16]

The standard response to such questions is to dismiss them as "philosophical" (or, that most heinous of biological heresies, "anthropomorphic"), not scientific, and to fall back on the economistic "system" with individual survival as its basic motivating fuel, the power train driven like that of any other economic engine by competition for scarce commodities — in this case, rank.

Equally preposterous, in my view, is the imputing of "competition" to the various and sundry plant species and communities that follow one another in vegetative succession. On a scarified piece of ground the sequence might be ragweed and crabgrass, to asters and

81

goldenrods, grasses, and blackberries, to aspen, basswood, and elm, and (over many years) to sugar maple, beech, and even hemlock.[17] It would be unacceptably anthropomorphic to see one such group of plants as, in effect, *preparing* the habitat for the next group of plants in a series — even though that is precisely what they do.

In studious avoidance of this unthinkable conceptual trap, ecologists (non-anthropomorphically) call the first plants to arrive "pioneers," "invaders," and "opportunists." All species through the process are called "competitors" for "scarce resources" as the community develops toward a hypothesized final equilibrium stage, or climax, "dominated" by a particular vegetative association. Plant species and communities employ various "strategies" throughout.[18] Such are the ways of value-free scientific objectivity, and such is the tenacity of de Candolle's botanical "state of war" of the 1820s.[19]

This is not to suggest that there is anything wrong with anthropomorphism (except that it is demeaning, somehow, to the animals); my complaint is addressed to those pots who call the kettle black. To see wild Nature as a competitive "economy" is to anthropomorphize — to ascribe or impute to the non-human, qualities or motives or attributes that are uniquely human. (But not quite. These qualities and motives and attributes are specifically those of the dominant Euro-American exotic ideology; they do not belong to all human cultures any more then they belong to non-human cultures.) In defence of anthropomorphism, however, it must be said that we have no real alternative. Being no more than human, we apprehend the world in human terms. My dogs apprehend the world in dog terms. They "canimorphize" *me*, as a member of their social organization. Neither they nor I discredit the other in so doing, however, and neither wants or needs to have it both ways.

No one denies that chickens, under distress, move into a precedence sequence. Neither does anyone deny that many species of mammals have analogous social arrangements, in which every individual has a place, or station, in relation to all the others. Some of these arrangements are extremely complex. Of the highly social species, none has come under more intensive or prolonged scrutiny than the primates.

Our closest living relatives are of great interest to physical and cultural anthropologists, taxonomists, palaeontologists, ecologists, psychologists, students of biomedicine, and many others. Usually the underlying motivation is curiosity not so much about them as about *us*. Apart from ourselves, living primates are the closest approximation available to what may have been the nature of some of our precursors. Not, of course, that we are "descended" (or, as some would have it, "ascended") from any of them, or that any modern primate is more or less "primitive" than any other, because all of us are contemporaries, but some of the modern forms may provide some clues, or at least intuitions, about the human primate. For these purposes the focus is on social behaviour.

Depending upon which authority you consult, there are 170 to 200 or more species of primates extant in the world. It follows that is foolhardy to make any but the grossest generalizations about them. Each has its particular biological inheritance, its particular ecology, including habitat, and thus its particular way of conducting its social affairs. Behavioural field-work has tended to concentrate on species that are either our closest kin (apes) or mainly terrestrial (baboons), or because habitat or some aspect of behaviour offers a degree of ease in observation (vervets, some macaques and leaf-eating monkeys, howler monkeys, etc.) The least studied are the small species of deep rainforests.

The easiest primates to observe, excepting ourselves, are those that are held captive. In a zoo, you can observe the living animals at close quarters, and write down what you see them doing. If they copulate or masturbate or fight, you write that down. If they do not do anything, you can write that down too. Chances are they *will* do something, however, because close confinement tends to cause prisoners of whatever species to behave in strange and often unfortunate ways. As in the confines of the cock-pit, bloody mayhem can erupt spontaneously. Once upon a time, zookeepers did not know this, and ferocious carnage would break out among baboons, for example. The scientific observers of the day were able to infer from such behaviour all manner of nasty and brutish primate dispositions, ranging from an aggressive drive for power to male dominance to social hierarchy — all, of course, rooted in the twin *a priori* and radical assumptions of competition and the pecking order, but rooted also, it must be said, in traditional (white Euro-American) male beliefs about the nature of gender roles in social organizations. Males fought for the power to dominate the social hierarchy, with the spoils (females) accruing to the victor, who was necessarily the fittest proprietor and governor, having won the competitive struggle. Believing is seeing.

Perversely enough, like the pecking order, hierarchical male social dominance, aggression, and the competitive lust for rank continue to infect and contaminate both scientific and popular views of Nature — and, by extension, of ourselves. A crucial phenomenon emerges here. As it is with the biologist who scorns and vilifies anthropomorphism, yet uses it daily, and as it is with the status-seeking/self-awareness paradox, the observer of primate behaviour can keep the options open. You may thus see aggressiveness as "natural" (following some of the writers of the 1960s) and an ineradicable part of human nature which needs no further explanation, *or* while still seeing it as "natural," you may choose to see the human animal as having transcended brute Nature by means of our moral and ethical systems. Either interpretation is available for instant application, depending upon the circumstances. It is this intellectual legerdemain that underlies much of the rhetoric of war, for example, much of pseudospeciation, and indeed most of the corpus of humanism. "Having it both ways" is one of the many gifts of human primate abstract rationalization.

For many years, primatology was dominated by white male Euro-Americans. Graduate students of either gender had little choice but to work within the accepted model of reality. It was Louis Leakey (who always described himself as a zoologist, not a palaeoanthropologist) who in the 1960s sponsored two students who were to become towering figures in field primatology, Jane Goodall and Dian Fossey.[20] Both loved natural history, as did Leakey, and both were born field-workers. Both also were very much their own women. I cannot but think that it was this last quality as much as their extraordinary talents that allowed them to pretty much stand old-line primatology on its head. Neither of them was ever to be entirely freed of the traditional male biases (competitive dominance hierarchy, etc.),[21] but by perceiving and accepting the chimpanzees and gorillas as *thinking and feeling individuals*, they changed their science forever. (It is entirely fitting that they were Leakey's students. He was no mean iconoclast himself.)[22] Goodall and Fossey were not clinically observing programmed automatons; they were subjectively and qualitatively valuing sensate, sentient personalities. This was new.

Neither, however, shook zero-order beliefs such as male dominance and aggression, hierarchical social structure, and territoriality. It remained for a burgeoning new generation of female primatologists to carry forward the heavy-duty subversion of the "dominance paradigm."

Where it had been taken as given that it was the aggressive competition of individual males that determined and maintained the structure of power hierarchies, the trail-blazing primatologist Thelma Rowell suggested that perhaps the behaviour of "submissive" individuals, not dominant ones, causes things to appear as they do.[23] This was an attractive notion. After all, it is the behaviour of the individual chickens in deferring to the "top" bird that allows us to identify her. Sometimes you can recognize "Alpha" in a group by his or her demeanour, but often not. It is much easier to observe the rank and file. The way they carry themselves and the way in which they behave will usually lead your eye to the central personage. The rank and file are behaving *in relation to* that individual. In a massed cheek-by-jowl reception at Buckingham Palace, you may well not be able to see the tiny Queen, but there will be no doubt where she is, as a deferential public swirls excitedly about her. Needless to say, such behaviour tends to reinforce the structure of any hierarchy.

The observation of "deference," although it does help to cleanse the mind of notions of constant individual competition for top rank, and violence in maintaining it, still leaves us with a hierarchical structure, even in the absence of any reasonable evidence. Take a gorilla band, for example. Gorillas live in relatively small groups of several females and young, and perhaps two or three adult (silverback) males (sometimes just one). Even where there are more than one, however, there will always be one whom we consider "Alpha," and in relation to whom the others consistently behave.

This however proves nothing whatever about status-seeking, dominance, or hierarchy, even though so many observers persist in perceiving them. One may suppose that in most cases the giant silverback had greatness thrust upon him. He may have drifted into a social vacuum (an unoccupied place) quite passively. Certain qualities — in this case, gender, age, and size — make it unnecessary for him to do anything at all. He may very well have "achieved" his position, but this should not lead us to suppose that he competed for it. It happened. It *had* to happen, in the interest of the social organization, that someone occupy that place, and he was it.[24]

86

One of the most attractive photographs of gorillas in the wild ever published is by Alexander Harcourt, one of Fossey's team members,[25] showing a very large male sitting in lush vegetation with females, juveniles, and infants clustered all about him. It is as though they cannot glue themselves to him closely enough — in this instance, not to seek his protection, because they are clearly not frightened, but rather for their pure satisfaction. Another such insight shines from a photograph by Kelly Stewart, another Fossey worker,[26] in which a gigantic silverback is sitting in the dappled forest glow with a tiny infant sitting behind him, back to back. *Closeness* to one's own loved ones is pleasurable; everybody knows that.

Physical protection or security can readily be inferred as the motivations of gorilla small fry, and no doubt there is some of that, but it seems insufficient to explain the fact that young animals are consistently *attracted* to the big males.[27] There are other examples. Male olive baboons, like male gorillas, are almost twice as large as the females. Until very recently it was the custom to see them as aggressive hierarchy-oriented dominators. They too are attractive to infants. In a troop of baboons at Gilgil in Kenya, then being studied by another primatologist, Shirley Strum (and known in her publications as the Pumphouse Gang), I was astonished and delighted to see one large male who was consistently swarmed over and played with by a group of very small fry. It was as though this particular male had an avuncular (or at least a baby-sitting) "role" which he relished. A male olive baboon, like a silverback gorilla, is a formidable creature. In spite of that, it would seem that peace and tranquillity play a larger part in the lives of both species than the aggressive stereotypes used to suggest.[28]

Yet both popular and (with notable exceptions) scientific works continue to demand that we see primate societies as bound together by a struggle for dominance in a rigid power hierarchy. The grey langur of south Asia is a case in point. This is one of the long-tailed (sometimes called leaf-eating) forest monkeys, in which linear male dominance hierarchy is usually described as the norm. Unlike most members of their family, these langurs often spend a good deal of time on the ground and in the open, where you can easily see them.

Although I claim no authority on the subject of wild primates, I have watched a good number of species in good a number of places. Once, having watched a society of grey langurs for several days, I was able to recognize some individuals. The troop consisted of about twenty-five members, of which three were highly visible adult males. These three communicated with one another noisily and vigorously, and pretty well continuously. During rare periods of silence, as when their mouths were stuffed, they would still keep watching one another. Then they would resume their mutual grimacing and chattering, and occasional chasing. These, by the book, were the "Alphas" of the troop.

Much more interesting than the behaviour of these adult males, however, was that of the rest of the group. Whatever they might have been doing at any given moment — eating, grooming, feeding young, resting, playing — they rarely took their eyes off those three males for more than a few seconds at a time. When the males became a little more vociferous or demonstrative than usual, everything else would be stopped instantly, and every member of the larger group watched fixedly, looking at each male in turn, with total attention.

All at once, I experienced a serendipitous[29] moment. It appeared to me that these interactions between the three adult males were generating some form of magnetic attraction which just might be a necessary element in holding not only everybody's attention but also the cohesiveness of the whole group. On this view, the Alpha males, so called, are not at the top rung of a hierarchical ladder; they are at the core of an encapsulating envelope around the social group. They did not have to strive or struggle for this role; like the silverback gorilla they merely happened to be the right gender and age as required in grey langur society to be the focus of attraction and organization.

This view suggests that the structure of the society is not linear but spherical. The group is a cell, not a pyramid, and the interacting adult males are at its nucleus. They are not *themselves* the nucleus; they are *at* the nucleus. Their energetic activity creates and maintains a central attraction for the group entity as a whole. That energetic "magnetism" is essential to the cohesion of the group, and it is the males' job to produce it. On this view, the social structure is built not on dominance and subservience, but on a dynamic of mutuality — a positive force analogous to whatever it is that keeps the individual atom or solar system from flying apart.

Over the several days in which I was able to watch these grey langurs, I did not see a sign of hostility between the males. There was plenty of wild and intemperate screeching and hollering, plenty of face making, and some sporadic chasing, always without catching, but no aggression, and no competition and no striving for dominance. This is not to say that fights do not occur between individuals, because they do. Also, male grey langurs at least occasionally practise infanticide.[30] Both have been part of the human primate story forever.

Fighting and aggressive competition for dominance in wild (not captive) social animals, when it does occur, can usually be charged to distress of some kind. Although theirs remains a minority view, Thelma Rowell and others have argued that when dominance-oriented internecine violence erupts, it may be seen as a pathological condition.[31] Crowding, food shortage, sickness, sudden environmental disruption of some kind, are among the possible factors. Another, at least occasionally, can be the presence of the human observer. Of the most overwhelming importance, however, is the

omnipresence in biology of the tyranny of the Darwinian interpretation of animal social behaviour. Believing is seeing.

Old cultural stereotypes die hard. The calcified rigidity of the
Western ideological prosthesis has totally resisted change until
very recent times. Only in the last twenty years or so have traditional images of a competitive male dominance hierarchy in non-
human species, especially primates, begun to be modified. This
has been largely but not exclusively the accomplishment of a clear-
eyed and open-minded wave of female (I shall not say "feminist"
for fear of being wilfully misunderstood) primatologists and
philosophers of science.[32]

Especially encouraging has been the long-delayed acknowledgment in animal behaviour studies that concepts such as "dominance," "rank," "status," and "hierarchy" are not absolute
realities, but *conceptual tools* for purposes of scientific observation, analysis, and communication. Primatologist Linda Marie
Fedigan provides these operational definitions:

> *Dominance... basically refers to some form of power over
> others established through intimidation.... "Dominance
> rank" refers to the relative amount of power over others in
> conflicts and conflict avoidance which an animal can exhib-
> it.... [A] linear dominance hierarchy is a straight-line rank
> ordering of animals* drawn up by the researcher *according
> to what are considered to be the animals' relative abilities
> to intimidate each other and thus win conflicts or use
> resources first [my emphasis].*[33]

Here we have a refreshing and forthright statement of scientific subjectivity — not the first, by any means, but valuable in its
contemporaneousness. Not only is the hierarchy inferred by the
observer, but also the observer uses certain subjective criteria
(power, conflict, rank, intimidation, winning, "resources") in mak-

ing that inference. It is clear that the traditional perceptual lenses have not changed.

The lenses have not changed because they are prescribed and ground within the ideological prosthetic device which dictates how we receive and apprehend the nature of reality. We *must* receive and apprehend the world through the bias of competitive striving because if Nature were *not* an economistic marketplace, then it would not be in our preferred image, and if it were not in our preferred image, then we would have no way of predicting and controlling it. We would have no way of domesticating it — of bringing Nature into the orbit of human power, of making it *just like us.*

Further, as we have seen, until very recent times primate research sternly maintained what can only be called a male-chauvinist model of animal social organization. It would not be inaccurate to say: just like ours. But as we have also seen, primate societies may readily be understood as peaceable and reciprocal extended family-centred aggregations of mutual interest. (Some are now known to be organized along lines of matriarchal kinship.) Such arrangements are not unknown in the human context. We may have much to learn — or to remember — from the social behaviour of non-human primates.

> *The mutual grooming of the primate horde and other hedonic linkages between individuals... provide us with a model for society, and incidentally for sexuality, other than the right-wing insistence on peck-orders and sexual dimorphism. Instead of expecting human societies to fall into hierarchical and sexist patterns, we can identify friendship as the central theme of the primate biogram.*[34]

Without changing the sense of the above in the least, I would add "compliance" to "friendship" and extend it to all social beings.

91

I shall offer only one further example of the reactionary nature of modern ethology. This concerns the culturally constructed scientific reality commonly known as "territoriality." Few gratuitous anthropomorphisms are more pervasive, or more pernicious. In its simplest sense, the notion suggests that many non-human animals seek proprietorship over a foraging or breeding area, that they actively compete for such physical plots or spaces, and that they aggressively assert their proprietorship against others of their species.

This variant of competition theory is a major supportive belief in all of ethology, and it is especially important in bird biology. The simplest definition of territory is that it is an area defended against others of the same species. Robins defend their territories against other robins, and orioles theirs against other orioles. But robins do not defend against orioles. The economistic interpretation of this is that the birds stake out a claim to a piece of physical property sufficient in size to provide resources necessary for the raising of a brood of young. Turf itself being a scarce resource, the acquisition of a territory is the result of aggressive intraspecies competition. Females are attracted to the owners of territories. After nesting is over and the young are on the wing, the need for a claim staked and defended against one's own species is over, and the territory is no more.

The territory is often defined, described, and defended by means of sound — vocal or instrumental. A male songbird has a number of selected singing perches surrounding his territory; he moves from one to the next, thus delineating or mapping his piece of physical turf for the information of potential mates and of his neighbours of the same species. If a neighbouring male intrudes, he is instantly and aggressively driven off. The owner of the territory always wins; the intruder always loses. This fiercely aggressive behaviour is most vigorous near the centre of the bird's territory, least so at its edges. Boundaries are thus evident: lines where the tension, as it were, is equally balanced between two adjacent proprietors.

This is the conventional interpretation of territory. It has a long, unbroken lineage that has been documented at least as far back as Aristotle.[35] The usual cultural values shine forth: aggressive competition and proprietorship over both physical space and females, winning and losing, rugged (male) individual enterprise. Every respectable text will tell you these things. Females are drawn to those males who have aggressively obtained a share of the world's goods. The more attractive the territory in terms of resources, the greater is the likelihood of its owner attracting a mate and raising a brood which will inherit those desirable competitive qualities. The defended area is seen as the bird's freehold *property*.[36]

No one denies that many species of birds breed in a nest-centred area which is also used by members of other species, but not by members of the same species as the nesting pair. The size of the area depends on the foraging needs and habits of the particular species. There is no doubt that such an arrangement is helpful in avoiding overuse of a particular habitat type by birds with identical nutritional requirements. Animals have a number of ways of avoiding the perils of overpopulation; this is one of them. It serves to space birds within their preferred habitats. Where the situation is ideal for a species, the nest-centred areas will be smaller, allowing more pairs of that species to participate; where it is poor or marginal, there will be fewer nests. All naturalists know these things.

Although the scientific interpretation of bird spacing "mechanisms" maintains the usual economistic bias, alternative constructions of this particular reality are possible. I shall attempt just one.

First of all, it just might be that the individual bird has no inherent lust either for competition or for the ownership of property. Both of these seem to be most unlikely attributes to project upon a bird. It just might be that what we call the bird's "territory" is

93

in fact the bird's seasonally adjusted *self*. Or, it could be seen as its seasonally adjusted "personal distance." The words do not matter; the images do. Neil Evernden has attractively illustrated this through reference to the much-studied "territoriality" of the stickleback:

> *It is as if the boundary of what the fish considers* himself *has expanded to the dimensions of the territory. He regards himself as being the size of the territory, no longer an organism bounded by skin but an organism-plus-environment bounded by an invisible integument.... It is as if there were a kind of field in the territory, with the self present throughout but more concentrated at the core.*[37]

Whatever image we use, the effect is the same — this year's stickleback or songbird brood successfully reared. It should not especially matter, then, what feelings or motivations scientists choose to attribute to the animals. After all, the procedure works. I suggest that it *does* matter, because our traditional perceptual stances on phenomena lead unavoidably to a single, unidimensional apprehension of those phenomena and, by extension, of Nature and the world. Just as the willingness of Goodall, Fossey, and so many of their successors to see individual apes and monkeys as thinking and feeling *subjects* brought a liberating new dimension to primatology, so a shift in our perspective on "territoriality" could benefit us further. As Evernden suggests, we might then be able to move to a new science altogether, "a biology of subjects,"[38] in which the focus of study would not be the animal as object, but the animal as *being*.

This might not be quite so difficult as it sounds. After all, we would be using the same evidence; no new data would be needed. The ornithologist's notebooks are filled with notations of what the birds did while they were being observed. It is simply a matter of putting the raw data through a different filter.

Take the interactions of two neighbouring male birds — let us say cardinals. There is between their extended selves what some might see as a demilitarized zone of elastic tension. On the current view, when one bird moves over the border the other drives him out. The intruder (who is the loser) retreats in fear before the aggressive reaction of the proprietor (who is the winner). One does wonder. Perhaps the neighbouring bird does not retreat before jealously proprietory anger, but rather *defers* to the resident's personal distance, which happens to be more extensive than usual. Perhaps he acknowledges and respects that encapsulated cardinal existence next door.[39]

Perhaps the cardinal social imperative is not competition but compliance. And of course it works both ways: when the roles are reversed the same compliant behaviour ensues. Perhaps the chasing interactions we observe between breeding birds are no more than exercises — dare I say *games* — which serve the individual needs of both participants. This conclusion may be reached on the same body of evidence that led us to perceive competitive proprietorship. The two interpretations are equally anthropomorphic, to be sure, but one is rational (quantitative and abstract) and the other is spontaneous (qualitative and participatory).

I emphasize again that both results are drawn from exactly the same field observations. The only difference is that, in the observer's notebook, for "competitiveness," we may now read "complementarity"; for "aggression," we may read "play." Dogs and antelopes and eagles and geese and monkeys and people play chasing games. Why not songbirds? Incidentally, songbirds such as cardinals also chase in the wintertime. The azimuth of the sun being what it is in January, we can be fairly certain they are not driven to aggressive competition by stirring gonads. Red squirrels also chase on the bright sunlit snow.

Let us, just for the sake of possibility, remove our culturally conditioned eyeglasses for a moment. Let us see the singing cardinal in the springtime as surrounded not by staked-out physical turf but rather (following Evernden) by a kind of invisible osmotic membrane encapsulating his temporarily extended being. In that case, the shrubs and trees and herbaceous plants and all the animals within that space are in the most real and literal sense built into his very existence — at least for a few weeks. In singing and displaying around the periphery of his greater self, the bird may be seen as celebrating, not his proprietorship but his *presence*, the phenomenon of his being. Extended as it is, his existence (in early June at least) includes very many other plant and animal existences — thousands of them. What is being celebrated, then, is community. The next time you hear a bird song, think of it as a conscious (and subjective) celebration of multispecies community participation.

(My editor, Jonathan Webb, has pointed out that "musth," the condition of reproductive readiness in male elephants, has been generally characterized by Western observers as the sex-craziness of testosterone-driven bulls. An ancient Sanskrit text, however, describes the state of musth as "an excess of joy" — a nice shift of perspective that fits very neatly here.)

The songbird's existence has miraculously become hugely greater than himself, incorporating as it does plants, animals, microorganisms, soil, water, and sunlight into his total being. We may take this even farther. The bird has himself become a community of existences, and at the instant when he sings, the momentary (once only) event of that song is numinous. The numen is not, of course, a presiding spirit of that place, external to the songbird; the numen arises from the mutuality or the complementariness of the bird and his co-participants. There can be no numen without this relationship, which is selfless, creative, and energetic. Mere

96

ego cannot have this quality or achieve this result, because mere
ego cannot transcend the individual organism. The quality derives
from the heterogeneity of uncountable participating existences.
And all of it happens in the *now*.

A number of birds sing duets, in some species the female and
male taking very different, intricately interwoven parts. This is
difficult to reconcile with the prevailing wisdom. Ornithologists
have been puzzled as well by the fact that many birds continue
to sing in the non-nesting season. Two white-throated sparrows
sang around our front yard all last winter. The songs were somewhat strangled and gargled and constipated, but they were perfectly recognizable. The cardinals also sing, on sunny days, and,
occasionally, the chickadees and woodpeckers and nuthatches.
As well, there is a phenomenon called the "whisper song" in which
the bird sings almost inaudibly, as though in the back of its throat,
so quietly that one must be very close in order to hear it. This is
fairly common in several species in late fall and winter. As with
the chasing, obviously competition for mates and land tenure have
nothing whatever to do with it. Nor does breeding condition. I
have speculated that perhaps the reduced personal distance of the
off-season might at times indicate reduced volume. And, perhaps
birds like to sing.

I have long felt that we so assiduously and unrelentingly spray-
paint upon Nature a lacquer of human motives, motivations, and
machinations in order that Nature may thus be made to seem to
resemble us sufficiently to be compared to us, with results inevitably
flattering to ourselves. When we are able to find in Nature competitive striving for personal status, jealous proprietorship by
males over females and real property, rigid hierarchical rank-order,
and naked aggressiveness, we may see ourselves, by comparison,
in a superior light. Yes, we do these things from time to time, but
that is in the nature of things. But — the ultimate clincher — we

are *aware* of what we are doing and of our reasons for doing it.

The ideology of human chauvinism requires "selfhood" to be kept in the human family. Non-human beings are mere striving "egos."[40] Much of Dian Fossey's difficulty with the conservation establishment in Europe and North America, for example, arose from her love (manifest in part by her recognition of the "personhood") of her gorilla intimates.[41] This was going too far. Some things are sacred. Give a lower animal a "self," and before you know it, some ideological subversive will want to give it a soul.

OTHER
SELVES

Of the sundry characteristics of the domesticated mammal set out in "Prosthetic Being," one of the most important is its loss of ecologic place. We may see this as the amputation of the fundamental skills required to play a co-evolved, healthy, contributory role in interspecies relationships. Worse, a domesticate run feral can play hob with that same community, as the Galapagos goats have done.

The loss of ecologic place applies to the total population of a particular kind of domesticated mammal. For the individual within that population there is the parallel loss of what I have called the sense of "at-one-ship" with other members of a community, and with it the awareness of "being-a-place."[1] The former term is meant to convey some of the quality of *wildness* in a multispecies natural situation, the latter the sense of *belonging* in one's home core.

The natural social organization of the animal having been dissolved, it is replaced not by a new interactive social order but by the one-way dominance of the domesticator. Some vestiges of natural sociality may remain, but these are consistently overridden by unilateral dependence. Intragroup social mutuality is gone; the individual has little relevance, even among its own kind. Any sense of relationship with members of *other* species — with the exception of the proprietor — has been removed. The individual can maintain interspecies community connections no better than we can. The social universe of the domesticate has become constricted; it has shrunk away not only from individuals of other species but also from those of its own. All that it is left with is its *self*.

The concept of "self" is an expression of dualism. It dichotomizes our world by requiring the additional concept of "other." The twin notions are mutually reinforcing. They are analogous if not identical to the conceptual human/Nature dichotomy. Both are part of the greater cultural tradition under which we labour, part of the prosthetic device which provides and sustains our ideologies.

The ideological prosthesis allows (indeed requires) us to undertake all the familiar rationalizing which goes into the poignant task of demonstrating the human transcendence of natural (animal) nastiness and brutishness. We usually transcend animal nastiness and brutishness through our moral and ethical systems. Such systems, and the smugly complacent warmth they kindle in us, not only feed our collective self-esteem but also help to maintain the cultural edifice of our emancipation from our own biological reality.

Few exercises in rationalization have involved quite so much intellectual pretzel-bending as has the task of demonstrating absolute human uniqueness. Our obsession with this is revealing. It's not enough that every individual, and every species, is a unique, one-time-only, event. Fanatical humanism demands more. All species are unique, we may acknowledge, but one species is *uniquely* unique.

100

Which reveals a good deal more than bizarre English usage.

Thanks to studies in ethology and behavioural ecology, the religion of human uniqueness has sustained a series of notable setbacks in our lifetime. We have had to abandon a substantial list of "unique attributes": tool using, tool making, language, tradition and culture, abstraction, teaching and learning, cooperating and strategizing, and others, less inflammatory, such as caring and compassion. There's not a lot left. But the ultimate fall-back position, the central jewel in the human imperial crown, had always been self-awareness. Then along came little Washoe.

Washoe, a chimpanzee, was raised by humans, Allen and Beatrice Gardner. She became famous as the first non-human being to learn the hand-sign language of the deaf and mute, a mode of communication seen by the Gardners as more useful to a chimpanzee (because of its anatomy) than human sounds.[2] While still very young she became extraordinarily adept in signing, which of itself generated concern in some quarters. An ape was not only "speaking," but also, apparently carrying on conversations with her human mentors. But Washoe's historic bombshell was kept in abeyance for a time. She had been supplied with various toys and other miscellaneous items, and had also become used to all manner of human household hardware, such as mirrors. One day, while she was looking into a mirror, she was asked "Who is that?" "Me, Washoe," she signed back.

Washoe was "self-aware." This was flabbergasting. And for many people it was deeply unsettling. We seemed to be witnessing the collapse of the last bastion of human uniqueness. Something had to be done about Washoe. Human brows furrowed in thought. Then came the answer. Of course! How blindingly obvious! Washoe was not *aware* that she was self-aware. One could almost feel the collective sigh of relief. We could not *know* this, of course, but it was fundamental to the shoring-up of the collective self-esteem

101

that we assert it. Now if it were somehow demonstrated that a non-human animal was, in fact, aware of its self-awareness, then, no doubt, the claim would be made that it was not, like us, aware of its awareness of its self-awareness. This could go on forever, and probably will.

The problem of self-awareness (or rather, the problem of our unrepentant claim, in spite of Washoe and others, that beings who are not human do not have it) confuses a number of issues pertaining to the human treatment of other animals. It appears consistently in defence of vivisection, for example. "Sentience" is much used as a synonym for self-awareness, or sometimes, consciousness. Non-human animals are not sentient (consciously self-aware); therefore, it is ethically permissible to do as we please with them. Such reasoning is mystifying. Even if the living, captive individual beings (both wild and domesticated) upon whom the vivisectors visit their incomprehensible acts were *not* self-aware, how would that justify cruelty? No one denies that they have central nervous systems (that is one of the important reasons they are used), that they feel pain (another reason), that they entertain fear (still another). Fear without self-awareness is gibberish.

Vivisection has its own strange ethical code, but it is not the only such structure to depend ultimately on the concept of self. Ethics rests on moral philosophy. Moral philosophy rests primarily on the concept of the individual. Presumably the concept of the individual rests ultimately on the concept of self. It used to be generally assumed that non-human beings were incapable of thinking or behaving ethically because, among other limitations, they lack the concept of self. That was pre-Washoe.

Many humanists attempt to handle the problem of self-identity in a chimpanzee by asserting that the animal lacks the capacity for *reason*, and therefore could never conceive of moral or ethical rights and obligations. That the animal lacks reason could be debated (there is ample evidence in many species of problem solving, which could only be conceptual). What the animals very probably do lack is the power of *rationalization*, which would appear to be a uniquely human attribute. Wild non-human beings do not require it because they do not live in a surrogate prosthetic universe conceived, crafted, and constructed on abstract invention. Their world is intact.

It is important to remember that Washoe was a tame, human-conditioned wild animal, not a domesticate. Her wild chimpanzee genes were fully intact. She had become initially the captive and later the associate of human beings, but she was not their artifact, not a behavioural amputee. It seems that she liked the Gardners, and had no reason not to. The friendships developed by Dian Fossey with wild gorillas make the point even more dramatically, as these animals were free to come and go, and to decide for themselves whether to accept her. Gentleness and affection were reciprocated by individual animals who were free, wild, and whole.

It is the wholeness of the wild animal that distinguishes it from the experientially deprived domesticate. It is the wholeness of the wild animal that makes ethical constructs unnecessary — indeed, probably unthinkable. Why create an abstract set of rules and guidelines when you are already doing all the right social things, and always have? Why seek replacement parts when you are complete? Rules and guidelines are for domesticates. Infantile, self-centred domesticates.

I conclude this not from scholarly research but from years of subjective experience, as a naturalist. It strikes me that the role of self in non-human beings is profoundly different from its role in human cultures — especially in the Western tradition. It seems to me that in our culture there is inordinate emphasis on the *individual* self,[3] and that individual self is inordinately emphasized at the expense of other modes of self which it is possible to see in non-human beings. Such beings are not the slaves of ideology.

Wild, free animals show no sign of the infantile fixation on individual self which so perversely is held in such high esteem in our culture. I do not mean mere rugged individualism, although that is a product of it. More important for these purposes is that the human individual is seen as the measure of all blessedness. Human groups, communities, and populations are blessed to the extent that they are aggregations of blessed individual souls, not as deserving entities in their own right. (Non-human phenomena are, of course, not blessed at all. As individuals, groups, and communities, they stand below the salt of self-sacrosanctity.)

Naturalists have difficulty with this cultural preoccupation with the individual. In full awareness of the role of the individual animal as a vector of genetic material, and in full knowledge also of its several contributory activities within the natural multispecies community, naturalists perceive in the demeanour of a wild animal less a self-interested single entity, more a manifestation of whole *being*. The naturalist sees a wild animal as one among uncountable ephemeral corporeal emergences, one minor miracle to remind us of the ineffable whole. It may be that loners, such as bears and tigers, are more evocative in this respect than are more gregarious beings. But even these are not usually seen as mere self-serving individuals; they are seen as revelations of bearness, of tigerness, of wildness.

In highly gregarious species such as flocking birds, the individual is lost not only to our sight but also to our awareness. As this page was being written, there were outside in the trees flocks of hundreds of close-packed common grackles, caught short in their spring migration by an early April snowstorm. In such a situation the idea of a single grackle, though conceivable, has no reality at all. The harsh grating cacophony of their voices, the noisy wave of flappeting wings in the snowy branches, bespeak the quality of grackleness. The individual grackle has for me no meaning — at least at this moment — whatever. One cannot help wondering whether (again, at this moment) it has any more meaning for the birds themselves.

This phenomenon is brought closest to our understanding by the movements of tightly packed flocks of migrating small shorebirds — sandpipers, for example. Take an aggregation of dunlins foraging on an exposed tidal mud flat. Their colouring being what it is, even a large number of birds can easily go almost unnoticed — until they take flight. Then, flashing pale wing-stripes en masse usually reveal that there were very many more birds on the ground than we had thought. But that is the least of the dunlins' disclosures.

As we watch the little birds in the air, invariably we marvel at their speed and their extraordinary manoeuvrability. Always, too, we stare astonished at the marvellous synchrony of their movements. All change direction together. Rarely, it seems, is an individual out of phase with the others. No matter how often we have seen it, invariably we ask ourselves how in the world a flock of these mites contrives to twist and turn and rise and fall in such near-perfect unison. The operative word here is "how." Steadfast in our subservience to the prosthetic ideology of how-to-do-it, immovable in our mechanistic and individualistic metaphysics, we ask *how the instructions are communicated.* How does the individual bird know what it is *supposed to do?* By what means are the necessary commands (the assumption of a "leader" is ineradicable) transmitted and received? And how can the individual bird act upon them so swiftly?[4]

These are good rational questions. The synchronous movements of the flock are much too rapid to be the result of simple follow-the-leader. There is clearly no leader. The birds are not strung out in linear file; they are massed, and act virtually as one entity. (In an exceptionally large flock you may see a slow twisting wave move from front to back, but even then the birds in any segment maintain perfect relative orientation, and internal changes of direction are as fast as before.) How is it done? A chemical cue is too improbable. Perhaps the "mechanism" (a much-loved word in biology) is a visual or auditory signal of some kind, beyond the capability of our sensory apparatus to intercept.

Perhaps — if only in the interest of human humility and mutual interspecies respect — it is time for us to acknowledge that we do not know what it is that determines the synchronous movements of a flock of shorebirds. We might consider — just *consider* —the possibility that this phenomenon is not mechanically based at all. Perhaps this is an aspect of being that is neither physical nor chemical, but rather one arising from what we call "consciousness."

But it does not arise from self-consciousness or self-awareness as we commonly know it. Our usual understanding of those terms is tied to the individual. It is difficult to imagine the instantaneous directional shifts of a flock of dunlins having been accomplished by scores or hundreds of individuals, each moving independently, after having received, processed, interpreted, and acted in accordance with some mysterious "signal." This would be too much. Instead I would suggest that there is at play here some form of awareness that is shared across the entire group. The flock may be seen as having one consciousness. The individual bird (at least in the flocking season) would lose its individual identity in that of the group. For a time at least, it would *be* the group.

This speculation is supported by the observations of anyone who has ever watched a school of fish — not from above, but on their own plane and at close range. The flashing angles, turns, slants, starts, and stops are too swift, too fine-tuned — indeed, too erratic — to be executed by the synchronized separate movements of hundreds of individuals. I have marvelled at this many times, among many species of fishes, and have felt that the school is not

106

a mere aggregation of individuals but a superorganism. It is composed of discrete physical parts, to be sure, but its behaviour flows from one awareness, one consciousness, one self. In a psychological sense at least, the individual *is* the group.

Flocking shorebirds and schooling fishes are highly visible manifestations of group self-consciousness. Most animals do not usually consort together in such densely packed congregations, and in any case the concentrations break down and disperse during the breeding season. At that time there is a change in the nature of self, to which I shall return. There are also species that gather together specifically for breeding purposes, and disperse thereafter.

This is the way of many seabirds. It has been suggested that, at least in some species (murres, for example), successful reproduction in a given year may depend upon the presence of a minimum density of breeding birds on site. When that critical mass is reached, a wave of sexual excitement moves through the colony, and the season's business commences. If for some reason the population of the colony falls below that critical level, the birds who remain may fail to come into breeding condition. It is as though the colony itself, not the individual pair, were the reproductive unit. The colony as a whole has its own physiological cycle, requiring a "trigger" to move it (the colony) into a reproductive mode. Like a flock of shorebirds or a school of fishes, a seabird rookery may be understood as it*self* an entity, one qualitatively different from a mere aggregation of participating individuals.

It is a little more difficult, but no less valid, for us to perceive at least a temporary group identity in other forms of coalescence, such as those of the social insects, or the winter hibernacula of some snakes, or large bat roosts. Families, whether nuclear or extended, of various primates, of wolves, of hunting dogs, and of elephants, all behave as though, at least most of the time, the group is of "one mind" about conducting its daily affairs. Loose cannons among their members are unusual. Such groups retain their cohesiveness under most circumstances. Individuals take minor forays beyond the shifting core, but are rarely out of touch. One way and another, the sundry parts of the greater whole keep in contact, as though maintaining the correct frequency to receive the behavioural consensus from moment to moment. A group consciousness prevails.

A group self becomes evident when one such party encounters or becomes aware of the nearby presence of another of its species. Responses in these situations are species-particular. Often noise making is involved. When two troops of howler monkeys or two prides of lions roar back and forth, it seems reasonable to assume that they are not saying "This is me" but "This is *us*." Wolf howling appears to be both intra- and interpack, holding one group together and simultaneously identifying it to another. No doubt the same or a very similar cohesion imperative is satisfied in much the same ways by individual pods of whales.

But what of those whose way it is to be loners? Take bears, for example. Bears are not truly solitary, of course; adult females are usually accompanied by their most recent offspring. Males tend to forage alone, except when there is a feast of such auspiciousness as to draw them together — a salmon run, a beached whale, or perhaps a garbage dump. Even though the animals do not ordinarily feed at such close quarters with one another, the richness of the bounty seems to offset any potential for quarrelsomeness. Usually such events are peaceable.

Even though bears do forage so widely under normal circumstances, they appear to have some uncanny way of knowing where other bears are in the general area. The human ecologist Paul Shepard and the English scholar Barry Sanders have put it nicely in their *The Sacred Paw*:

If socialization is defined by living in packs or year-round mate association, then bears are solitary. But perhaps the net of bear sociality is cast so wide that primate observers like men, with their poorer senses of smell and hearing, cannot appreciate its subtlety and scale. If bears have in their heads a constantly revised map of the locations of other individual bears, should we not then consider them as truly socially oriented?[5]

Both whales and elephants appear to be able to keep in touch over considerable distances by means of sound, using frequencies at or beyond both the upper and the lower limits of human hearing. Must we see these scattered solo bears, whales, and elephants as merely roaming individuals, or could we not accept them as comprising strands or knots in Shepard and Sanders's "net" of sociality, and by extension an unusually widecast but still coherent entity?

This brings us toward Neil Evernden's evocative metaphor of "fields of self."[6] The image of a field or a net of barren-ground-grizzly-beardom on the arctic tundra renders unnecessary and somewhat wrongheaded the attempt to force-fit the grizzly into a preconceived category of sociality. Individual bears are not so tightly coordinated in their movements as individual sandpipers, to be sure, but the difference may be one of degree, not of kind. Since biologists, as humans and like dogs, are socially cooperative animals, their form of being is seen as more "highly" evolved than that of the bears. Much of the study of non-human animal behaviour is riddled with such tacit human-chauvinist moral judgment.[7]

In suggesting the existence of a group self, a group self-awareness, and a group self-consciousness, I am down-grading the role of "other" in the social life of individual wild, whole beings. I am suggesting that the everyday consciousness of such beings, rather than being centred on the individual self, may be transcendant and *participatory*.[8] This is not to say that the widely postulated role of "other" is done away with at this level, because it may be seen, if we wish to see it, in the two howler monkey groups roaring in concert.

What is being suggested here is that individual self-consciousness has come to be held in such untouchable esteem within our cultural ideology that we have largely forgotten or ignored the likelihood that it is no more (or less) than the most basic, radical, and fundamental form of self-awareness. Yet it has been elevated to such a pinnacle of dominance that it used to be the ultimate and unchallengeable criterion of humanness. That was before Washoe. Ironically, that claim may well be accurate after all. Perhaps a consciousness limited to individual self *does* define the human species. Terrible thought, but it is hard to believe that we would have survived, in evolutionary terms, so crippling a disability.

The fact the human animal is not extinct suggests that our difficulty with self is the result of cultural conditioning rather than biological inheritance. It could be confidently argued that in the course of our cultural (not biological) evolution, we "traded off" more sophisticated, more mature, more adaptive, more ecologically appropriate appreciations of consciousness against our sacred individuality.

Individual self-consciousness (self-awareness) may be not only the most basic form of consciousness, but in an evolutionary sense also the oldest and most "primitive," to use a word beloved of the humanists. I would suggest that this most radical form of consciousness underlies more enriched and mature forms in much the same way as the ancient so-called reptilian brain is said to underlie more recently developed cortical material. If we must speak in sequential terms, as is the custom in evolutionary biology, then we could see a consciousness of group-as-self as something of a development.

But we *need* not see it that way. Individual self-consciousness serves an indispensable function for the newborn, for example.

The newborn, as a sentient being, must presumably have some reference point for all that follows, and no doubt individual self is just that. But that isolated individuality is soon subordinated to the greater reality, which is that of the immediate family. Gradually the infant's self-centredness metamorphoses into the consciousness of the group — or at the very least, the parent at hand.[9] Over time, the infant ceases to see itself as the core of a self-centred universe (or perhaps as the total universe), and begins to perceive itself as participating in a family-centred universe. Where the process moves from there would depend entirely on the biology and the ecology of the species in question. For bears, it is a loose arrangement; for primates, something tighter; for yellow-jackets, something tighter still. For many species the influence of this form of consciousness waxes and wanes with the seasons.

We now arrive at a plateau which is a good deal more challenging. Beyond the consciousness of self-as-group could be posited a consciousness of self-as-community. Perhaps the word "self" need no longer be used here. As we have seen, the role of "other" has already diminished as we entered the envelope of the group consciousness. At the level of the community, "other" is bereft of whatever abstract meaning or utility it may have had. In the functioning multispecies community, all participants are subjects; objective perception is no longer required with which to receive the world. There need be no other; the community is a whole unto itself.

This level may be seen as problematical because when we set aside the concept of individual self we are at the same time abandoning the usual concept of "interest." In conventional domesticated thought, interest, like "other," is a necessary corollary of self. The economic bias of competition-oriented ecology would have considerable difficulty in finding anything *but* self-interest in the behaviour of individuals, species, groups of species, associations, and communities. Such is the case because, as we have

111

seen earlier, self-interest (the seeking of personal goals) is the basis of the economic model on which ecologic and evolutionary interpretations rest. Neither convention is tenable without it. Both, however, must necessarily remain at the individual level in order to sustain the goal-orientation of competition theory.

Paradoxically, ecology deals chiefly with the complex interrelationships between species and groups of species in associations and communities. It rarely addresses organisms as individuals. The individual may be invoked as an abstraction in the defence of competitive "niche" theory, for example, but at best only as a unit, at worst, a cipher. Ecology is most comfortable at the level of populations.[10] Yet the structure of competitive theory rests ultimately on the "given" assumption of the struggling and striving individual non-human being, to whom self-awareness is generally denied.

If ecology were to award self-identity to groups and populations of species it might be more persuasive in its attribution of self-interest to wild Nature, and the implied function of the invisible hand in the natural marketplace. But this — ironically — it cannot do. That there can be no selfhood in non-human beings remains a fundamental tenet of the Western prosthetic ideology.

The most fundamental premise of ecology is that all things natural are interrelated. In theory at least, nothing occurs that does not affect everything else. The concept of competition is easily maintained within this broad framework, but so, of course, are concepts of mutualistic cooperative reciprocity and interdependence. The latter terms, however, are usually reserved in ecology for relationships among particular species, while competition is applied universally, from the individual outward.

While ecology is able to conceive of (biological survival) "interest" residing in a group of social beings (a family of otters, a colony of gannets, a den of mongooses), and perhaps in the local population of a species, that interest is understood only in the mecha-

112

nistic-reductionistic terms that system analysis demands.
Quantitative, "objective" science is unable or unwilling to accommodate the concept of organisms' subjective interest in their personal well-being. Self-interest may be acknowledged — but only
grudgingly — to the extent that it can be measured within a com-
petitively constructed calculus.

It would seem undeniable, however, that the aggregate of the
populations of all of the species (which is to say the community)
inhabiting or (more accurately) comprising a prairie pond or a man-
grove island or an alpine meadow or a beech-maple-hemlock stand,
has an interest in the continuance of that association. If the individual has a consciousness of its self-interest, as it most certainly
does, and if that consciousness is extended to include the group, as
it appears to be, then surely it is a very short (perhaps inevitable)
step to individual awareness of self-as-multispecies community,
with that awareness shared in common by all participants.

If all of the individual beings in a community share that total,
greater consciousness, then it is not unlikely that they may see individuals of their own and of neighbouring species not as "others"
but as simultaneous co-existences or co-expressions of that place,
perhaps as extensions of themselves. Surely the browsing deer and
the grazing hare do not find it necessary to objectify their herbage
clinically, to draw some abstract dualistic differentiation between
themselves and some vegetative "other." They *are* what they eat,
and before they eat it.

When a fox draws a bead on a meadow vole, or a green-backed
heron lines up a leopard frog, is the "intentionality" involved any
whit different from that of a skunk digging white grubs or a tad-
pole nibbling algae? The dust-boiling, crunching, thumping impact
of a lioness striking down a hartebeest is identical in kind, identical as a *phenomenon*, to the quick sharp selection of an inchworm
by an oriole. Neither requires the objectification of "other." Every

species has a particular method of obtaining its food. Eater and eaten are equal co-participants. Each *is* the community.

A coyote chases and catches a cottontail. This is a simple and discrete event involving two individuals. One attempted to obtain, and did so. One attempted to escape, and did not. In the course of the chase, both were propelled by self-aware motivations. Over those few seconds, the only consciousness in either mind, I should think, was that of individual self — basic, fundamental, radical, and simple. Group and community consciousnesses were set aside. But only momentarily. For one participant, his rabbit self-awareness is no longer necessary; he has become coyote. He might have become great horned owl or red-tailed hawk or long-tailed weasel, but coyote is as agreeable a destiny as any. For the other, her immediate task accomplished, group consciousness returns with a rush; she trots denward with supper for her puppies. Later, in the evening, coyote singing will celebrate community being. Rabbits will hear, shrug, and go about their own participation.

As interpreted here, individual self, group self, and community self in wild (whole) beings should not be construed as mutually exclusive, nor indeed (except in the specific case of the newborn) as either sequential or hierarchical. It is more likely that all three forms of consciousness are present in all wild beings at all times, and that a particular mode may be called upon for temporary emphasis according to the exigency, opportunity, or requirement of the moment or the season.

It would poorly avail the coyote to go hunting in the individually self-conscious configuration. She would find little; community self would seem to be indicated for that purpose. When she spots the rabbit, she shifts down to the lowest individual self/other range only for as long as absolutely necessary to catch it — a matter of seconds. With her group and community self-awareness suspended, even for so brief a time, she is exquisitely vulnerable. Usually, she gets away with it. It does happen, however, that coyotes rapt in individual contemplation occasionally become wolf, or cougar, or bear. From the point of view of coyote genetic self-interest, that is probably just as well.

It is possible to postulate a fourth level of consciousness of self, a wider sphere of the awareness of personal involvement than the group, or even the community. Many wild beings do not live for the entire year in one community, or even in one *kind* of community. Migrants may breed in one type of habitat and spend the off-season in another. Some travel immense distances; to the human observer, such undertakings are mystifying, because suitable conditions often are available that would require a fraction of the investment in time and energy. Terns, shorebirds, fishes, and some whales all come to mind here. Why *bother*?

Clearly, migrations are related to optimum food supplies in both breeding and resting seasons. Movements between two places are regarded as traditional (some would say they are "programmed," that the animals are "hard-wired," but I do not know what those terms mean, as applied to sensate beings). Tradition, though a comfortable concept, actually tells us very little about what may be going on in the collective mind of the migrants. That there is usually some measure of urgency involved is fairly clear, although some species do loaf their way along with no apparent concern about tomorrow. This is as it should be; living is about the *now*. But twice each year, *now* becomes the time to move.

There are almost as many explanations for the timing of migrations, and for the routes taken, and for the navigational accomplishments of the animals, as there are migratory species. All are interesting, but none is of much use in our attempt to understand what is going on within the being (both individual and group) of the participants. Since such questions are not seen to be within the proper purview of science, conventional interpretations, whether they use the word or not, generally hinge on "instinct." As Gregory Bateson delightfully pointed out in one of his "metalogues," instinct, like gravity, is an "explanatory principle" which explains everything and nothing. Such a principle is "a sort of conventional agreement between scientists to stop trying to explain things at a certain point."[11]

No burden of quantitative explanation will be assumed here. It is possible, however, to speculate upon the quality of the common experience that is migration, the shared consciousness of the immediacy of a primal imperative and the need for its satisfaction. The onset of migration usually coincides, or can be argued to coincide, with local meteorological or oceanographic conditions.[12] Those conditions do not originate locally; they are the products of planetary weather and climatic patterns which are themselves influenced by gross topography and the rhythms of the celestial bodies. Migration is a biospheric and solar affair.

To credit the onset of migratory stirrings in animals to some yet to be fully understood physiological cycle is simply not good enough. There is *awareness* involved, and that awareness is shared across the collective participating consciousness of the population concerned. Cues come in to the individual, the group, and the community (mixes of many species are often involved at both ends and during the journeys). Those cues are local interpretations or particular versions of greater regional, continental and planetary promptings. Wild, whole beings would appear to have full sensibility not only to local signs, but also to the greater orchestration which they themselves will now perform.

It may not be preposterous to suggest a consciousness of biospheric self. Such a form of self-awareness would be transcendent — independent of the necessarily material context of individual, group, and community. But in moving beyond these, the biospheric self would not replace them. Rather it would subsume and

116

hold them precious, as vital and integral domains, or types, of the greater whole. None is expendable. Very likely, freely willing immersion in both group and community self is a prerequisite for the individual experience of the whole. Awareness of whole self is emotional, not rational. It is an event, not a construction. It is experienced, not known. It is lived, not abstracted. It is received, not perceived. It is a gift, not an accomplishment.

It is possible to understand the biospheric self as shared in the consciousness of entire populations and communities, perhaps building at critical times in their cycles and their lives, receding at other intervals when recourse to other forms of self is more appropriate. The preliminary "restlessness" and mounting excitement before the onset of spring and fall migrations, wet and dry seasonal movements, and breeding periods would all seem to relate to the apprehension from beyond the immediate community of a quality of self-awareness different in kind from those involved in workaday affairs. A similar "feeling" may be heard in the songs of wolves and whales and toads, seen in the aerobatics of ravens, the sporting of dolphins, the chute-sliding of otters, the bathing of elephants. It may be felt also in the individual human "peak experience" of any sort, at any time.

We call such experiences "peak" because of both their rarity and quality. Magnificently performed great music may occasionally induce it in some of us. (This has importance because it is derived not out of our usual overreliance on vision-cum-abstraction but rather out of our given and much-neglected capacity for auditory pleasure and satisfaction.) Some of us are similarly transported by the spring songs of birds, the fall grunting and whistling of wapiti, the staccato of raindrops on lily pads, the cracking of lake ice. The sound of winter wind in the leafless aspens is the experience of being-the-whole. The smell of skunk-cabbage is good too.

I believe that in spite of our cultural conditioning and domesticated ideological dependence, as living beings we still have simultaneous access, if we will it, to all four states of self-consciousness: individual, group, community, planetary. In theory at least, we all retain the capacity for wildness. In practice, we cling limpet-like to the ideology of dualism, we deny the virtues of wildness, and we deny its accessibility to us. Our unrelenting denial of the need for experiential nutrition, together with its consequences, is the burden of the following chapter.

KIDS' STUFF

I have referred to the "experiential undernutrition" of the domesticated animal. By that I mean its failure or inability to assimilate to any significant degree the experience of self-as-group, while self-identity as either multispecies community or biosphere is beyond it altogether. It cannot benefit from the experience of entities beyond itself, and thus it cannot mature as a fully sentient and participatory being. This is understandable. The qualities we most admire in wild animals — their alertness, vigour, sensory acuity, self-sufficiency, ecologic fittingness, interdependent sociality, attachment to a place, individuality, and all the rest — are precisely those we most disfavour in our living artifacts. In the interest of their predictability and controllability we have gone to great lengths over hundreds — even thousands — of years to "breed out" of our domesticates the qualities of wildness.

The result of our careful selection of breeding stock has been a

119

group of animals utterly lacking (save the dog) any sense of either social or community (interspecies) place. I have described such an animal in the previous chapter as having little or no apprehension of any social universe beyond its *self*, and have heaped some opprobrium on such a condition. It is not, of course, the individual animal's fault. We made it what it is. We manufactured it in our image.

It has been pointed out that although domesticates grow very rapidly, they never really grow *up*. That is exactly the way we want it. Unfortunately, if one measure of growing up is the achievement of group, multispecies community and planetary self-consciousness, then neither do we. Where the domesticate has been genetically manipulated into that parlous condition, however, we have not. We are the creatures of our ideological prosthesis — the surrogate for wild wholeness that allows us to believe in our separation from and supremacy over Nature. Though the animals' plight is genetic and ours is ideological, the net result is strikingly similar. The development of the young domesticate is arrested by the nature of its physical being; the development of the young human is arrested by cultural conditioning.

In *Nature and Madness*, Paul Shepard diagnoses the failure of self-development in Western society as the cause of our environmental destructiveness. Much of his account consists of a merciless Western psychohistory at the sociocultural level, but he includes a provocative (epigenetic) theory of human child development, introducing it in this way:

> *In the ideology of recent times — of progress and the self-making of the person and the society, of the ego's selection of choices of what-to-be, appended to a body — the child is a* sac physiologique *that is fostered and that grasps or obtains thought and intelligence.*
>
> *Epigenesis is a contrary concept of life cycle (or ontoge-*

ny). The person emerges in a genetic calendar by stages, with time-critical constraints and needs, so that instinct and experience act in concert. The mature adult is a late stage in this lifelong series of overlapping and interlocking events: not linear but spiral, resonating between disjunction and unity, but moving, so that each new cycle enlarges the previous one.[1]

The developmental process, as Shepard explains it,[2] consists of a series of three "bonding" events at three matrices. Following each bonding event the individual cuts loose from that matrix toward autonomy, then swings back to bond to the next. "Mature individuation requires successful passage through three bondings and three separations." The first separation toward autonomy is birth. The first bond is to the mother (Matrix I). After venturing from infancy toward childhood autonomy, the child then swings back to the second bond, which is to Nature (Matrix II). At puberty, the third bonding event is to the cosmos (Matrix III). The autonomy of adolescence, all three bonding events accomplished, points toward individuation and maturity.

Shepard observes that

Matrix I [bond to mother] is fundamental and provides the basic paradigm. Matrix II [bond to Nature] is the least understood. It embraces the child's fascination with nature, his spontaneous enthusiasm for the names and natural history of plants and animals, and the soaking-in-a-place which makes it the basis of the intuition of an orderly universe. The religious concepts of Matrix III [bond to cosmos], and the language used to describe them, depend on metaphors from the first two levels.[3]

He emphasizes that this "complicated passage through separations and symbioses is human and primate. It evolved. It is based on an extended life — extended not only by time added at the end, but by an expanded youth."[4] It is specifically human; it is a biological, not a cultural, imperative. Since it is a sequential process, each stage building on the preceding one, any interruption or frustration of the process will "stall" the development of that individual at that stage. For purposes of this essay, the critical accomplishment is at Matrix II, the bonding (symbiosis) with the rest of Nature.

Although Shepard's theory is confined to individual human development, I suspect that the stage of bonding to "Nature" — to the entire multispecies community — is common to most mammals and birds. Indeed I cannot see how *any* animal could function without it. It is the basis of wildness, the platform for entry into that "real world" that transcends the individual. The relative duration of this phase varies hugely across wild animal species, and in some may be barely noticeable, but it is there, to the extent that the life history of that species requires it. My confidence in this rests, on the one hand, on the clear and indisputable integration of wild species in natural communities, and, on the other, on the well-known failure of interspecies integration and the patent destructiveness of domesticated forms. The latter, on this definition, have not realized Matrix II.

The domesticated being cannot undertake or consummate that bonding experience. Its sensory apparatus is too restricted. Even the obvious mechanical items such as scent, hearing, vision, and tactility are in varying degrees crippled. From the outset of its life the animal is poor at processing even the meagre sensory information available in its simple, monotonous environment. The typical barnyard animal seems largely unaware of or indifferent to even its immediate surroundings. It is this general absence of sensibility that makes the hoofed domesticate such a poor candidate for the achievement of any bond beyond its ephemeral attachment to its mother.

The four forms of self-consciousness (individual, group, community, biosphere), although inspired in part by Shepard's bonding theory, are not congruent with it, nor do they represent an analogous developmental process. Those self-awarenesses are seen as being simultaneously and spontaneously available to the mature, wild animal according to the dictates of the moment, and all are resorted to in its daily life. This unencumbered access to alternative forms of self-consciousness is critical for any being, because it reflects its ability to function as an appropriate and contributory participant in the world.

Bonding is a relatively recent concept, and remains poorly understood. We have long known about marriage bonds and family bonds and bonds of fellowship, but the notion of bonding as a *process* is quite new. It implies the seeking and the realization of a psychological *attachment*. The need to bond is presumably "innate." As Shepard uses the term, it is an essential element in the development of the mature individual. It may or may not be reciprocal. In the case of a close-knit gorilla or hyena society, clearly the bonds are mutual. In the case of the individual bond to Nature, or to the cosmos, conscious reciprocity is not required. The process consists of individual acceptance of a greater sense of being.

In natural history and biology, the concept of bonding is less familiar than the related phenomenon of "imprinting." In the common usage, bonding is *active* (one bonds oneself *to* something), imprinting is *passive* (one *is* imprinted *on* something). In a more critical sense, the distinction is fine, because both are accomplished by the initiative of an individual being. In practice, a behavioural biologist (trained to use only the passive voice in the interest of objectification) will freely speak of the known fact of imprinting, but will likely be uneasy with "bonding" as we are using it here.

This is no doubt because imprinting may be expressed mechanistically, while bonding has a disturbing taint of the mystical (and perhaps of non-human "selfhood") about it.

As an idea, imprinting belongs to the twentieth century. It belongs originally to ornithology, having first been noticed in bird behaviour. It is generally seen as a form of what I would call "experiential" but science calls exploratory or latent learning. The word was coined by Konrad Lorenz in the 1930s, but it had been known for some time that newly hatched ducklings and goslings, for example, will follow and "fix" upon the first large moving object they see. In Nature, that object is almost always their mother, who usually "leads" them to the water within a few minutes of hatching. It had been noticed, however, that if the first moving object in their experience was *not* their mother, they would follow and fix on it anyway. The most likely candidate for the birds' "mistaken identity" would be a human being who had kept the eggs in an incubator.

Indeed the target of the little birds' attachment need not be a living being at all. Experimental psychologists and others have caused newly hatched ducklings to become imprinted on inanimate objects moved across their field of vision: wooden duck decoys, cut-out duck silhouettes, and other paraphernalia from alarm clocks to footballs. This is not as cruel as it sounds; unless it is systematically reinforced, the attachment wears off shortly. In Nature, the imprinting on the parent was required only long enough to get the hatchlings safely into the water and launched on the multifarious learning experiences of the rest of their lives.

In cases when the deception *is* reinforced, as when a newly hatched bird is tended and reared by human individuals, and has no continuing experience with its own kind, it may well come into full adulthood and sexual maturity with certain inappropriate intimate expectations of human beings. This had been known for some time before the embarrassing lesson had to be learned again by the keepers of whooping cranes in an early captive breeding program. Taking the whooping crane fiasco to heart, staff at the San Diego Zoo recently fashioned a food-dispensing puppet in the rough image of an adult California condor in order to keep little zoo-hatched condors on the right track toward their possible eventual release to the wild.

Lorenz, who popularized this phenomenon by means of films, articles, and his famous book *King Solomon's Ring*, had flocks of geese following him about, attached less to each other than to him, even as adults. No doubt he maintained the link by caring for them himself. This we might properly see, in birds more than a few hours or days old, as a continuing form of deliberate conditioning. They were not geese being force-fed to enlarge their diseased livers, but they were geese being psychologically malnourished toward an eventual identity crisis. While the primary function of imprinting is to ensure the young birds' safety over the first few hours of their lives, a parallel function would appear to be to instil in them the ability to recognize their own species. The individual bird is learning, as it were, that it is a goose, not a duck, and that it is a grey lag goose, not a bean goose.

The experimental objects of Lorenz and others, and the victims of accidents such as the sexually misdirected whooping crane probably do not "think they are people." It is more likely that they think people are birds of a feather (thus committing the sin of ornithomorphism), whether or not they know that they themselves are geese, or cranes. Whatever may be going on in the minds of the individual birds is less important than the fact that they are imprinted. The underlying imperative is described by the ornithologist Carl Welty in these terms: "Briefly, the adaptive significance of imprinting seems to be to gather the extremely impressionable and vulnerable young around a tutor who immediately begins to teach them the hard facts of survival in an unfriendly world."[5]

Imprinting is not confined to waterfowl, or to birds, for that matter. Nor is it confined to the visual sense. It may be accomplished by sound, or by scent, or by taste, or, no doubt, by tactility, depending on the natural history of the animals involved. There is often a considerable expenditure of effort on the part of the young animal. In the case of ducklings, experiments revealed that "those birds which made the greatest exertions to follow the decoy [over obstacles] made the highest imprinting scores."[6]

This would not, of course, apply to young songbirds, raised in the nest and unable to run about and follow a tutor. They would make a different kind of effort and at a different time in their development. No doubt the way in which imprinting is done is as varied across species as any other element of their life histories. But every young sentient being *must* experience it, in one form or another.

A recent discussion of imprinting dismisses it thus: "The most obvious definition of filial imprinting is that simply because of being exposed to a certain type of object a young chick or duckling develops a preference for its company and comes to direct filial behaviour toward it."[7] Such a comment derives, I suspect, from the reluctance of mainstream psychology to admit imprinting as "associative learning" (putting two and two together). Whether imprinting requires putting two and two together I do not know, nor does anyone. More important is that conventional mechanistic science will reject, whenever and wherever it can, abstract learning processes in non-human beings. It might not be too far-fetched to speculate that imprinting as "latent learning" is so described in order to downgrade it as not worth serious study. This might be seen as avoidance of the *real* problem — fear and dread of the implications of non-human "associative learning," to say nothing of non-human "selfhood."

There are many animals for whom parental care is slight, or absent altogether. This must not be allowed to elicit a moral judgment on our part. Certainly, for a great blue heron or an arctic fox or a human being to abandon and not care for its young would be anomalous. But there are many animals, even vertebrates, for whom it is not necessary to exert "normal" parental attention. Little snapping turtles hatch in their sandbanks safe and secure, and go their way; little polliwogs hatch in their ponds and commence feeding; most little fishes do the same. There are even little birds who hatch in beach-pits like those of sea turtles; there are others who are born in warm compost heaps especially constructed for them. None of these animals requires an attending parent, and none is a lesser being for that. For such as these, the first species-specific imprinting (or bonding) event will no doubt involve their siblings.

No one knows what is going on in a little animal of those species that fix on and identify with a parent. Something impels the gosling to follow that moving object and "attach" itself to it. Something causes the downy wood duckling to find its mother (by sound) and then to follow her. (Wood ducks nest in holes in trees; when the little ones jump out they usually land in dense ground cover where vision is not much help.) Something encourages the human infant to seek and then to recognize its mother's breast, hands, and face. However initiated, the bonding is accomplished almost immediately by the ducklings, who are precocial ("born running"). The "premature" human infant takes a little longer; most species fall somewhere in between.

But before the newborn can find and fix, it must seek. In order even to begin to seek, a newborn would need to have an appetite, or a thirst, or at least a curiosity to explore its immediate surroundings. It would seem to want to investigate, toward some end. The finding of the parent is no doubt the first satisfaction of a child's life — the first nutrition for its whole psychological and physical development. Mother's milk is the second. The primary hunger is for the *experience* of bonding. In the course of the experience, Matrix I of Shepard's model having been accomplished, the young social being is already moving beyond individual self-centredness toward group self-consciousness.

Young, growing animals eat a lot, but their appetite for experiential nutrition is even greater. Watch any backyard puppy, kitten, or toddler, and you will see naked, unabashed insatiability for exploration and discovery. Especially, you will see the attraction of anything that is *different from* the little one's usual experiential fare. All three are visibly attracted to worms, crickets, caterpillars, grasshoppers, and butterflies. These phenomena are all small and unthreatening, and they move, but not so quickly that they cannot occasionally be caught. They can then be handled, smelled, rolled about, and tasted.[8] They can be experienced.

It seems that, for the bonding to Nature to be consummated fully, it needs to take place in pre-adolescence. The somewhat tentative and unfocused venturings of the toddler stage develop in later childhood into full-blown curiosity, fascination, and total involvement with phenomena that are not human. Every parent knows the incessant, obsessive questions that characterize this stage. We are asked "What *is* it?" and we are asked over and over again. The *naming* of things seems to be fundamentally important.

There are those who describe the naming ("labelling") of elements of Nature as a form of "power trip" on the part of the namer. This is no doubt accurate in the context of abstract scientistic taxonomy and systematics, but such activities are different from the intimate personal experience of wild Nature. The former requires objective removal ("standing outside"), where the latter is participatory and subjective.

Most of the time we find ourselves in the scientistic configuration; there is really no alternative to labelling if that is the only device left to us with which to attempt to comprehend Nature and to communicate our discoveries. Wild, non-domesticated animals, however, do not require a technical prosthesis in order to understand their own contexts. They are *born* surpassingly good naturalists.

When I identify a bird song as that of a wood thrush, I am thereby not only demonstrating my skill and knowledge but also my ability to categorize the animal, thereby reducing it to an inanimate cipher within a greater abstract taxonomic classification.[9] It is equally true, however, that when I learned the song of the wood thrush in my childhood, the bird became my familiar and my friend, who through my life reminds me of his presence with his voice. It pleases me to welcome the old friend returning after a long winter's absence. If I did not know who was singing, there could no doubt be some aesthetic appreciation of the sound, which unlike many bird songs happens to be euphonious to the human ear, but there would be none of the intimate pleasure of personal re-cognition. My childhood experience of the bird, and its lifelong annual reinforcement, ensure that each spring's re-cognition of our relationship is more satisfying than the last. What I celebrate is not merely the existence of the wood thrush, however; it is my *connection* to him. My bond to him. My self in him.

Very little is known about the childhood experience of Nature; few people have looked into it and even fewer have tried to understand it. One of the few who did was Edith Cobb; after more than forty years her contribution[10] remains the necessary point of departure for anyone who would explore this phenomenon. Cobb set out to show that human "genius" ("the high point of achievement in human growth potential") is rooted in "the child's perceptual relations with the natural world." Her interest in "genius" need not concern us here; what is important for these purposes is her exploration of "the spontaneously creative imagination of childhood" as it is served by the experience of non-human Nature.

Cobb suggests that the very prolonged human childhood allows

*plasticity of response to environment.... This plasticity may
be extended through memory into a lifelong renewal of the
early power to learn and to evolve.... [C]ertain aspects of
childhood experience remain in memory as a psychological
force, an elan, which produces the pressure to perceive cre-
atively and inventively.... Creative and constructive mental
processes do not result from an accumulation of information, but from the maintaining of a continued plasticity of
response of the whole organism to new information and in
general to the outer world.[11]*

I would emphasize "the whole organism," the total being. Cobb
is talking about *quality* experience in childhood. That quality, I
think, can arise only from a *heterogeneous* environment. (Wild
Nature is of all things heterogeneous.) Such is not the experience
of most domesticated animals. We make certain of that. A plasticity and spontaneity of response to diverse and varied natural
stimuli is the last thing we desire in our domesticates.

According to Cobb, "there is a special period, the little-under-
stood, prepubertal, halcyon, middle age of childhood, approxi-
mately from five or six to eleven or twelve... when the natural
world is experienced in some highly evocative way, producing in
the child a sense of some profound continuity with natural processes."[12] She says that what is at work here is an "innate appetite."
I take this to be similar in quality, or kind — perhaps identical —
to the appetite that causes the newborn to seek, to find, to fix, and
to bond. The need would appear to be equally basic and fundamental. The pre-adolescent seeks heterogeneous *experience* with
non-human phenomena of all kinds as essential nutrition for its
further development into whole maturity.

In this context, nutrition is more than a figure of speech. If the
child literally builds such quality experiences into its whole present and future being, then the child is nourished thereby through

the ontogenetic process toward mature belonging and thus participation in the world. The cross-species encounters of childhood,
having become part of the whole organism, persist and may be
recalled and re-experienced through later years.

We commonly hear of the evocative qualities certain works of
art have for individual people. A particular piece "never fails" to
produce some ineffable emotional response. All of us have these
— a snatch of Coleridge or Poe, a bit of Ellington or Borodin, a
phrase of Robeson or Fitzgerald, an expression by El Greco or
Augustus John, and very many more, that we cannot usually experience without the precise stimulus. But they are there, whether
through retrievable association or not. They are part of us. For
some, they may include great architecture, or notable vistas ("land-
scapes"). Still others among us respond to certain kinds of natural communities — swamps, marshes, prairies, ponds, forests,
seashores. There are even those who are triggered to inward ela-
tion by particular non-human *species*. Perhaps it would be more
accurate to say that they are stimulated by awareness of the *presence* of those species, however manifested.

My response on hearing the first wood thrush of spring is an
example. I referred to the celebration of *connection*. It would likely be better to describe it as the annual celebration of *reconnec-
tion*, not only to the wood thrush, but also to one's halcyon middle
age of childhood, the time during which the thrush became an
inseparable part of the whole organism that is one's multispecies,
community self.

There are elements of ritual in all this. One need not be embar-
rassed by that; all animals indulge in ritual — even domesticates.
All seem to require it. All seem to be nourished by it. In elaborat-
ed human ceremonies, ritual usually becomes prescribed, and
imbued with formal meanings. Non-human ritual, on the other
hand, may be seen as ceremonial without catechism, as participa-

tion without role, communion without obeisance, self without other. Re-cognition without abstraction.

When the wood frogs begin to quack in early spring, small patches of rotting ice often linger on their pond. There is a smell about rotting ice and meltwater that is the unmistakeable prelude to the voices of the frogs. No doubt one has learned to connect a certain scent in the air with wood frogs; I know that my skin and my nose tell me when it is time for them, and their first insistent little clackings are rarely a surprise. The fact that, where I live, the wood frog's singing season often lasts less than a week makes it all the more precious; on those occasions when I have missed it, I have known palpable hunger and frustration. A ritual so deeply and lovingly engrained cannot be interrupted lightly. Quality is always fragile.

This ritualistic attraction to the annual advent of frog song is an appetite every bit as insistent as that which prompts the newborn to seek and to bond, or that which impels the child to "devour" the experience of newly discovered non-human phenomena. As I have already suggested, the appetite would appear to be at least partly to relive the quality of that early experience. I believe it may also be a thirst for the renewal of one's own participatory *wildness*, an urge to be once again set free, however briefly, from domesticated servitude — to momentarily set aside our ideological crutches and to be whole.

That experiencing of this quality is so uncommon in human adulthood is testimony to the efficacy of the cultural indoctrination to which we have been put. We are conditioned not merely to be "civilized" (qualitatively separate from and superior to Nature) but also actually to be *proud* of that lonely ecopathological condition. Nature is kids' stuff, we say. They will outgrow it; after all, *we* did. We adults are concerned with "matters of consequence," as the Little Prince's businessman put it.[13] Institutionalized cultural downgrading of the experience of Nature makes it all the more difficult for us, as adults, to regain and recover the sense of transcendent self. It follows that for us to rejoin the wood frogs, even fleetingly, takes a little bit more than momentary caprice. As R.D. Laing says,

> As adults we have forgotten most of our childhood, not only its contents but its flavour... capacity even to see, hear, touch, taste and smell is so shrouded in veils of mystification that an intensive discipline of un-learning is necessary for anyone before one can begin to experience the world afresh, with innocence, truth and love.[14]

In a time of hands-on computer training for grade schoolers, there will be more for future adults to unlearn. Since keyboards do not dirty those exploratory little fingers or soil those designer running shoes, and since monitors display matters of consequence, we are now able to cause our children to bypass altogether the muddy, uncivilized propensities of the halcyon middle age of childhood. In a single atavistic leap of more than half a millennium, we will once again perceive children not as ontogenetic treasures but as short people. This is conscious conditioning, not only of our own perceptual inventory, but also of the children themselves, as domesticated living beings.

Children, like all domesticates, may thus be seen as the *artifacts* of high-tech civilization. The reader will no doubt have noticed in educational institutions at all levels the pervasiveness of the word "training." This is no accident. Indentured as we are to the ideology of how-to-do-it, we are able to see the world, including our own children, and including Nature, only in instrumental terms. Reflecting on this, and related matters, George Grant observed that technology has become "a package deal of far more fundamental novelness than simply a set of instruments under our control. It is a destiny which enfolds us in its own conceptions of instrumentality, neutrality and purposiveness. It is in this sense that it has been truthfully said: technology is the ontology of the age."[15]

If the nature of being may be understood only through the cosmological filter of technology, then we, and our children, and Nature, *are* technology. The Hereford steer is not only the product of technology, but, by extension, technology itself. Similarly, for the pre-adolescent the experience of technology is substituted for the experience of Nature. Rather than being permitted to devour (and become) polliwogs and cabbage butterflies, the innocent is fed (and becomes) the rational binary logic of keyboard and screen, mouse and joystick. *Nintendo, ergo sum.*

For the child who has bonded with and thus *become* non-human Nature, and who retains the capacity to retrieve that self-identity through adulthood, the wilful, deliberate, and conscious wounding of Nature is impossible, because that would be self-mutilation. Everyone knows that self-mutilation is crazy. For the child denied that experience, however, the mutilation of Nature may be wrought without the slightest inhibition. It is only natural to reshape Nature, as the child itself has been deformed, toward the manifest destiny of the technological imperative.

The arresting effects of experiential undernutrition on the development of children in urban-industrial society are made worse by the additional influence of chronic *mal*nutrition. To put it crudely, our young are fed too little organically produced food, too much junk food. Where the experientially *under*nourished child may be seen as a casualty of neglect and deprivation, the experientially *mal*nourished child may be seen as the model achievement of the process of domestic technological fabrication. Most of our society's children suffer from both. It would seem that while effects of undernutrition can often be ameliorated through proper doses of appropriate dietary supplements, the work of chronic malnutrition is much more difficult to correct. Where the former is a mere quantitative problem, the latter is one of kind.

Nature is complex and multispecific; the human environment is essentially simple and monospecific. True, there may be trees and shrubs and gardens where people live, a scattering of squirrels and starlings and pets, and sun and rain and snow, but the overwhelming presence is that of ourselves and our fabrications.

This is most easily demonstrated in terms of the *sensory* nourishment we receive in urban concentrations. Virtually everything we see, hear, smell, touch, and taste is of our own making. Worse, most of it is not even delivered to us by people; the bulk of nutrition for our senses is mediated by machines. A teenager sits on a concrete slab, feet resting on asphalt, eyes closed, hands clutching a plastic case, breathing swirling exhaust fumes, a headset piercing and battering both eardrums with screaming, shattering dissonance at a frightening decibel level.

Everything this youngster sees, hears, smells, touches, and tastes is a human artifact. His unidimensional experiential universe is one homogeneous, monospecific mass, with not the slightest differentiation. His sense organs, blunted as they are, need not be able to discriminate in any case; there is nothing to discriminate *between*. There is searing colour, to be sure, and cacophony, and heat and cold, and there are strange metallic flavours, and surfaces smooth and rough, and there is terrible, unending *qualitative* sameness.

Across the street there is a "park" (a rectangle of mown lawn). On a bench lies a derelict, inert, unconscious and oblivious, his empty grail of solace in its brown wrapper on the grass beneath him. As a child he may have encountered Nature. He may have once been wild. Perhaps he still is. Overlooking him there is a gigantic edifice of glass and steel, with guards and security video monitors and air-conditioned seven-dollar-figure condominiums with chrome strips and tinted windows and mirrored walls, and with live beings actually inhabiting them. Behind, in a brick-walled protected enclosure, there is a children's playground, with brightly painted climbing and crawling structures of metal pipe, padded with something made from synthetic polymers. There are sensate beings here, too. Little ones.

I have described elsewhere[16] what I call a kind of urban "sensory deprivation," and the perceptual (and thus conceptual) aberrations that follow from it. When perceptual and conceptual aberrations are shared across a society, they may be seen as institutionalized delusions. There are many of these in contemporary society, but none is more important, or more ironical, than the belief that high-tech urban "progress" (i.e., emancipation from non-human environmental influences) is a major human achievement. R.D. Laing has said, "Human beings seem to have an almost unlimited capacity to deceive themselves, and to deceive themselves into taking their own lies for truth."[17] It would appear that we have travelled so far in our cultural self-deceit that we actually believe we have no need of sensory stimulation or nutrition beyond that provided by ourselves. No need for experience of any influence that is not of human design and fabrication.

Our willing (and indeed prideful) confinement within the many-mirrored echo-chamber of technological servitude is a towering irony, perhaps the ultimate in self-deceit. Like the feedlot steer in the dreary monotony of his experiential desert, we have lost all connection with being, all memory of the sensibility of life context. Unlike the steer, we have expended monumental creative and other intellectual energies, and have consumed incalculable numbers of other sensate existences, in order to achieve full domesticated status. That status is fed, sustained, nourished, and reinforced by a synthetic diet in which ideology is substituted for experience. I call that ideology "zero-order humanism."

ZERO-ORDER
HUMANISM

There have been many varieties and shades of human chauvinism. For these purposes I am interested less in the relative merits of humanist arguments, more in the intensity and exclusiveness with which they all focus on the human miracle. All things beyond the species in the spotlight are lost in the blackness of irrelevance and unreality.

In one obvious sense, this is natural. Presumably all living beings use themselves as points of reference in dealing with the world. No doubt ostriches apprehend the nature of things in their relation to ostrichness, muskrats through the filter of muskratness. They enjoy ostrich and muskrat spotlights, respectively. However, if the ruminations of "Other Selves" are close to the mark, ostriches and muskrats, and other non-human beings, do not insist on being solo acts. They are in the centre of their individual spotlights, but if they are indeed possessed additionally of community and biospheric self-consciousness, as I suspect they are, then they *share* their self-focused universes with all of those who comprise them. They have little talent — or, indeed, time — for obsessive narcissism, which in Nature has no "survival value."

Presumably the universal imperative of continuing to be is central to ostrich awareness. The ostrich runs, after all, at the approach of a lion. So would you and I. It seems doubtful that the ostrich would consider it *wrong* in some ultimate sense to be captured and consumed by lions. But we would. Humans are too important to be wasted as cat food. Humans have consequence in the world. They have *potential*. The world exists for the advancement of the human project. The human project is first among Earthly — indeed, universal — meanings and purposes.

This peculiar notion is intimately related to our human technology. Even in early gathering and hunting days the collective human self-esteem must have been enhanced by our developing skills in the storing, retrieving, and transmitting of how-to-do-it, especially as those skills were increasingly manifest in the extension of human power over other species and whole communities.

As the domesticates of technology, we developed traditions and modes of behaviour, and ideas, that best served our master. As dependence upon our domesticator deepened and broadened, our ways of thinking mirrored the nature of that dependence. Our visual specialization and our hand–eye coordination fed both our success in the fabrication of things and our emerging dependence on a particular intellectual process. It is very difficult to draw a line between storable, retrievable, transmissible how-to-do-it and what we now call "reason." Reason *is* how-to-do-it: essentially, how to infer from fact or logic. We are the domesticated creatures of technical abstraction.

Now, many animals engage in abstract thought. There is all manner of evidence of non-human beings, from pigeons to chimps, baboons to octopi, addressing problems conceptually. The difference is that they do other things as well — interesting, useful, often beautiful things. We, however, tend to do very little else. Even aspects of our lives that used to be at least occasionally spontaneous — exercise and recreation, learning, eating, sex —must now be done by-the-book. We are even told how to "birth" and to "parent" by numbers, and how to die.

As we moved more deeply into conditioned servitude to reason, rationalization, and technique, the role of experience in our lives inexorably diminished,[1] ultimately to be subordinated almost entirely to reason. Our hyperspecialization was deftly rationalized from unprecedented domesticated dependence into unprecedented species chauvinism. Crudely put: if you've got it, and you're stuck with it, flaunt it.

Humanism is an ideological phenomenon only, a socially fabricated metaphysical crutch to the use of which we have been culturally conditioned for millennia. As living, sensate, and sentient beings we have no biological need of it, but as the psychologically domesticated creatures of custom and belief systems we need *something* to lean upon, and humanistic ideology is what we have been given. Perverse and unnatural though it is, human chauvinism nonetheless dominates and governs whole societies, cultures, and civilizations. Thanks to our technical and reproductive accomplishments, humanism also determines the fate of all of Nature.

By far the most penetrating — merciless — analysis of humanistic ideology has been that of David Ehrenfeld, who for his purposes describes it thus:

> *Setting aside the notion of human worth and dignity, which is part of many religions, we come at once to the core of the religion of humanism: a supreme faith in human reason — its ability to confront and solve the many problems that*

humans face, its ability to rearrange both the world of Nature and the affairs of men and women so that human life will prosper. Accordingly, as humanism is committed to an unquestioning faith in the power of reason, so it rejects other mythologies of power, including the power of God, the power of supernatural forces, and even the undirected power of Nature in league with blind chance. The first two don't exist, according to humanism; the last can, with effort, be mastered. Because human intelligence is the key to human success, the main task of the humanists is to assert its power and protect its prerogatives wherever they are questioned or challenged.[2]

The "religion of humanity" is celebrated not merely in the "humanities" (as contrasted with the sciences), but also in the sciences — indeed, in virtually every aspect of our intellectual, social, and cultural lives. Reason is heady stuff. As Ehrenfeld has shown, its uncritical worship has spawned and sustained a human arrogance that has had terrible consequences. (We may not care to see ourselves as part of Nature, but when at last we have brought the temple down, even the most dedicated humanist, were one present and sifting though the debris, would no longer be able to make the distinction.)

By "zero-order humanism" I mean something more than a "religion of humanity." One can, after all, opt in or out of a religion. The zero-order phenomenon is even more profound. It is manifested in the religion of humanity through the customary infallibility of reason, but it is less a creed, more an ordained *imperative*. I define it as "the ideology of the necessary primacy of the human enterprise." I describe it as "zero-order" as a way of emphasizing its quality as an unchallenged "given," an unwritten precept from which flow all other varieties of human chauvinism.

If the human purpose is *necessarily* primary in the order of the universe, then everything else follows, including the role of reason in the realization of that purpose, and indeed the role of institutionalized religion in sanctifying it. God need not be dead for this humanism. The human purpose is God's purpose. Those who do not wish to invoke God, however, need not. Even if the universe is indifferent to or, perish the thought, hostile to humankind, and all of us are on our own, there is still no doubt about the necessary primacy of the human endeavour. Zero-order humanism embraces all. Although the mythology of human necessity in the universe is sustained by prosthetic systems of belief, the physical enterprise itself is subsidized by Nature. On historicist evidence at least, that is the way it was *meant to be.*

This is the most overwhelmingly important myth in our cultural inheritance. According to Northrop Frye,

> *Mythology is not a* datum *but a* factum *of human existence; it belongs to the world of culture and civilization that man has made and still inhabits.... [T]he real interest of myth is to draw a circumference around a human community and look inward toward that community, not to inquire into the operations of nature.... [M]ythology is not a direct response to the natural environment; it is part of the imaginative insulation that separates us from that environment.*[3]

Clearly the myth of the necessary primacy of the human enterprise performs that function surpassingly well. As a factum, it rests upon and supports a multitude of other fabrications. This is a symbiotic model of mutual aid that in spite of its purely ideological abstraction has immeasurable power in our lives. The defensive stockade it maintains about our systems of ideas is comfortingly opaque. Within its protective walls it allows us to celebrate human reason to our hearts' content without being distracted by the light of experience.

141

Frye's description continues thus: "Myth has two parallel aspects: as a story, it is poetic and is re-created in literature; as a story with a specific social function, it is a program of action for a specific society. In both aspects it relates not to the actual but to the possible."[4] The myth of zero-order humanism is not merely re-created in the imaginative literature, of course. As everyone knows, it is fundamental virtually throughout the arts ("cultural") community. Much more important in practical terms, it is reinforced daily and ubiquitously in the language and literature of science and technology, of politics[5] and geopolitics, of social criticism, of business and finance, and of modern planetary "development" and management.

The governing mythic ideology is a program of action relating to both the actual and the possible. There has been a clear-cut agenda, at least since the Renaissance,[6] which in our own time has reached its fullest expression. In characterizing the ideology of the primacy of the human enterprise over all other considerations, I do not use the word "necessary" lightly. The icy humanistic intellectuality of Teilhard de Chardin[7] has now been recycled in the more contemporary technocratic idiom of the Gaians[8] and their many followers, and in such multinational "development" exercises as *The World Conservation Strategy*[9] and the Brundtland Report.[10] The goal is the humanization of the planet, the process is necessary, and is justified — indeed, sanctified — firmly and unequivocally for the advancement of the human enterprise.

The sacrosanctity of the human program is immune to challenge. It is zero-order. Critics of "sustainable development," for example, are expected to be silenced by the ultimate "trump card."[11] A trump card carries its own moral authority and, like any other absolute, requires no explication or justification. On the basis of already existing evidence, the destiny of Earth as a human monoculture is manifest.

Pre-eminent in the necessary prosecution of the humanization (domestication) of Nature is the role of science and technology. The chauvinism (indeed, the cultural despotism) of science and technology in our time receives its legitimation from two sources. First, there is the basic human dependence on an external agent of control (how-to-do-it). Second, there is the sanctity of reason, especially as it is exemplified in reduction and quantification. Science and technology are the heirs apparent and ranking princes of the humanistic faith. For the incumbents of positions so exalted, *hubris* is rarely far away.

In the 1920s John Dewey was moved to express his concern about the effect of scientism (not his word) on "the art of knowing":

> *The failure to recognize that knowledge is a product of art accounts for an otherwise inexplicable fact: that science lies today like an incubus upon such a wide area of beliefs and aspirations.... [T]he real source of the difficulty is that the art of knowing is limited to such a narrow area. Like everything precious and scarce, it has been artificially protected; and through this very protection it has been dehumanized and appropriated by a class. As costly jewels of jade and pearl belong only to a few, so with the jewels of science. The philosophic theories which have set science on an altar in a temple remote from the arts of life, to be approached only with peculiar rites, are a part of the technique of retaining a secluded monopoly of belief and intellectual authority.*[12]

That science and technology occupy the dominant place in our cultural hierarchy is exemplified in the imperial position of modern medicine. Medicine is mystical, mythical, magical, magisterial. It is beyond all criticism. It is not infallible, but its *agenda* — its program of action — is consecrated by the ideology of the necessary primacy of the human enterprise. As the very personification and embodiment of zero-order humanism, medicine towers above all other realms of science and technology in our society.

This is because medicine stands for one thing. It is *against death* — against human death, that is. Medicine is engaged in the subjugation of human death, which is another way of saying the mastery of Nature. Now, most physicians of my acquaintance are against human pain and suffering as well as human death. But the medical *establishment* — or, if you like, the industry — in which they participate presents itself as I have indicated without the slightest equivocation. On any given day in a Toronto subway car I can read advertisements placed by foundations dedicated to the vanquishing of particular diseases. Such advertisements tell me how many people will die of that disease this year, and where to send money.[13]

I already know that a great many people will die this year, but I have never been able to bridge the synapse between that simple fact and the need to send money. If I send money, will these thousands upon thousands of people not die, or will they die of something other than the ailments advertised? If I do not send money, will more people die of these causes and fewer of other causes? The logic has always escaped me. Life, after all, is fatal. I have often wondered what the medical industry would prefer I die *of*. It is abundantly clear, however, that no foundation wants me to die of *its* disease. Certainly I do not want any of my loved ones, or myself, to die in protracted agony. If the subway advertisements were to say to send money for palliative care in terminal cases, or to finance legislative lobbying for legal euthanasia or human population abatement, I would send money. But I have no money for the humanists' undifferentiated, total war on Nature.

Pleas for the advancement of the medical conquest of Nature are most often cast in the context of research. "Research" is another of the self-justifying shibboleths in our society. The rhetoric surrounding research funding, especially in biomedicine, is mysteriously vague on some points. Surprisingly often, we are not told what the research is *for*, except that it is "for" a specific disease. What is meant is that it is for research into the amelioration, control, or eradication of the effects of some malady. Rarely are we told what the researchers want to do, and, almost never, how they intend to do it.

In addition to this "goal-directed" research, insofar as its goals are actually articulated, there is the matter of "pure" or basic biomedical research, not necessarily directed at any particular problem, but rather toward the biological fundamentals, the way living beings and their chemistries, physiologies, and psychologies function. An example would be the phenomenon of *pain*, in the experimental study of which the researchers appear to be endlessly engaged. A great deal of this relies on experimental studies of individual non-human beings.

Individual beings used in this way are usually referred to as experimental "subjects." Were they in fact subjects, of course, they could not be used, because in the zero-order lexicon that would make them human. Non-human beings used in research are objects. Indeed it has happened in this century that human beings were also experimental objects. The notorious Dr. Mengele of the Nazi chamber of horrors was no doubt inspired and sustained at least in part by zero-order Aryanism — the ideology of the necessary primacy of the "Aryan" enterprise.

In point of fact, Mengele need not have hated Jews in order to do what he did. He need only have pseudospeciated them. By perceiving a taxonomic gulf between himself and Jews, he could view as necessary their role in his particular program, and their fear, pain, and suffering as an externality. He need only have seen them as animals. Animal experimenters in biomedical research presumably do not hate animals. But they see them as being in the necessary service of their particular programs, and their fear, pain, and suffering as an externality. The rationale is identical in Nazi chauvinism and broader human chauvinism. Superiority (power) confers privilege; lesser beings are by definition in the service of the higher purpose.

It is not my intention here to recount acts of viciousness perpetrated in the name of medicine that for sheer callousness border on the inconceivable.[14] What interests me in this context is less the nature of the perpetrators, or even of the society that endorses them, more the cultural mythology that gives them reason for being. I do not mean either the moral nature of what they do or the nature of their moral arguments in defence of what they do.[15] I mean the edifice of human-centred chauvinism that sustains them ideologically.

At the root of all this is the element of necessity. Most legislation having to do with the control of cruelty to non-human beings hinges on what is deemed "necessary" cruelty. Individual animals must not be tortured unnecessarily. We are never told what constitutes necessity. Nor are we told what criteria are used to arrive at a conclusion of necessity — such matters are left to peer review committees who meet in closed session. But, above all, necessity itself — as an idea or principle — is not open to discussion. As a concept, however, necessity is not an absolute; it cannot exist in a vacuum. Necessity arises out of certain circumstances which dictate whether a particular course of action is required, or a particular event is inevitable.

Since cruelty to sensate and sentient beings is scarcely inevitable, necessity must represent a required course of action. Here it will help to recall Frye's description of myth as a program of action relating not to the actual but to the possible. In biomedical research at least, if it is possible, it is necessary. It is not difficult to identify the mythic structure from which this strange imperative derives. If it is in the human interest, it is necessary. Even if the human interest extends no more widely than that of the research team or institution, that is sufficient justification. After all, there is nothing at stake but money. Like tongue depressors and Petri dishes, animals are materials to be used and garbaged as necessary.

The old truism "If it can be done, it must be done" is more than a popular slogan. It is an expression of unswerving domesticated fealty to ideology. When we add to that the sanctity of medicine in the advancement of the human enterprise, we have at least part of the explanation for such atrocities as the use of chimpanzees in AIDS research.

The AIDS epidemic is a natural response to human overpopulation and hyperdensity. Other species of animals, when faced with a population crisis, must either reduce or suspend breeding (which we will not or, as domesticates, perhaps cannot do), emigrate (there is nowhere left for human surpluses to go), starve (we have begun to do so), or fall victim to communicable disease. Clearly a disease that is sexually transmitted is the most efficient, because it eliminates the need for a vector (mosquito, rat, flea, etc.). Although diseases such as malaria are coming into their own again after temporary set-backs (the mosquito becoming "resistant" to insecticides, the plasmodium to drugs), from the point of view of human population ecology venereal disease has no peer as an agent of control.

Sentiments such as these are offensive to many people. They "objectify" the human phenomenon, holding it up without its gauze wrappings of myth and rationalization. Such objectification reduces us to the level of animals, and that is not acceptable to zero-order humanism. The human enterprise is *different*. The entire worldwide apparatus of medical technology must be cranked up to meet this latest challenge from obdurate, recalcitrant Nature. And no cost is too great to pay. There is some slippage, however, in the cost evaluations. Salaries and hardware are factored in; non-human terror and agony are not.

When the experimenters brutalize, torture, and kill animals in their laboratories they use the word "sacrifice." Since self-immolation is not likely to occur to any mouse, tabby, or beagle, there are only two possible explanations for its use. Either the experimenter believes in the appeasement of the gods through the ritual killing of animals, or someone's moral self-worth is being sacrificed to the higher endeavour. In the case of AIDS, chimpanzees are being used as "models." (A model is an abstraction or representation, a design or pattern; a living being is none of these.) Chimps were chosen because their chromosomal structure is close to ours. They are intelligent, sociable, trusting, defenceless. They are objectified (transmuted into "models"), infected with AIDS, then monitored.

At the time of writing, I have not known personally anyone who has been afflicted by AIDS. No doubt I will. But I have lost a long list of friends of my childhood and youth to another pathology of humankind, one in respect to which politicians are wont to utter the word "sacrifice" once a year, as they stand in front of the war memorials. Wars, whether on nations or diseases, depend on cannon-fodder — young men and boys, mice, tabbies, beagles, and chimpanzees, each with individual self-awareness, fears, susceptibility to pain and suffering. Cannon-fodder is an aggregate of such individuals. But after all, we are told, it was *necessary*.

It is at this stage that the devout zero-order humanist will move to identify the author as a hypocrite of the highest order. No one, it will be said, could have reached the age of threescore years and ten without having been the beneficiary of medical knowledge deriving from animal experimentation. This is to put me on the defensive.

My answer is simple. Yes, of course I have received medical attention through technology originally developed by vivisection. Most of us have, and almost all of us do. But had that technology not existed, I would have been none the wiser, and would not have been able to bemoan its absence. You cannot mourn the inconceivable. Few of us lie awake of nights fretting about the absence of human brain transplant technology, or even about the absence of fountain-of-youth technology. We refer ourselves to that which exists, and go about our daily business. Were animal experimentation to stop tomorrow, we would never know what we were missing. Had I been born a hundred years earlier than I was, many and wonderful would have been the medical phenomena that I would have missed. But I would not have known that. In my innocence, I would have proceeded as I now do — in innocence of what miracles may or may not obtain in future.

A much shorter answer to the same point — that I have had the benefits of animal experimentation — is that past cruelties do not justify present or future cruelties. That would be neither ethical nor logical.

Zero-order humanism, like all ideologies, is vulnerable to both ethical and logical analysis because its final bulwark consists of nothing more than its trump card. Remove the justifying moral authority of any manifest truth, and you have very little left. Remove the mythological "imaginative insulation" that surrounds a human society, reveal the world outside the cultural stockade, and — presto! — good things can follow. If the human enterprise can be shown *not* to enjoy primacy over all other things — and certainly not necessarily — then there could be positive consequences for all concerned. Perhaps even for the laboratory victims.

The decline of the fashion fur industry, at least, is encouraging. Public sentiment in North America and Europe has been turning away from the luxury trade in animal skins. For a number of years many nations have banned trade in the skins of threatened or endangered species, such as the spotted cats, but the current popular trend against fur is not a matter of the status, or the conservation, of the species concerned. An aspect of applied zero-order humanism, in this case commerce in the hides of mammals brutally killed for the purpose, is in the process of being dismantled. Fashion fur is increasingly seen as repugnant and unacceptable.

The general reaction began when anti-sealing campaigners brought to public attention photographs and films of the spring slaughter of white neonate harp seal pups on the ice of the Gulf of St. Lawrence. The spectacle is a sorry and hideous one, consisting of clubbing, skinning, and blood. Mostly blood. Eventually, the European Community took action against the importing of sealskin products. Again, this had nothing whatever to do with conservation; there are lots of harp seals. It had to do with the way in which sealskin was obtained and brought to market. There was no issue of "resource" depletion; there was only the issue of human sensibility. More important, it was an instance of *cross-species* sensibility.

People empathized with seal pups and their deprived mothers. Previously, concern for individual (usually domesticated) animals had been almost exclusively the province of humane and other animal welfare societies. Resource conservation cannot espouse the cause of individual beings, because resource conservation deals in "stocks" and "inventories" and "harvests" of free animal commodities. Concern for the fate of the individual harp seal pups represented a totally new dimension in human relationships with wild animals. The pups were not "resources"; they were feeling, thinking, suffering animate beings, viciously attacked, killed, and butchered in the interest of a frivolous commercial cause which fewer and fewer people found defensible.

The Canadian government, always the stoutest defender of received zero-order ideology, sprang to the defence of the seal industry, sending their own lobbies to Europe, enacting regulations to prevent the public from observing the annual slaughter, hiring professional public relations experts to discredit the organized public protest,[16] which soon encompassed the commercial fur industry as a whole.

In its initial stages, the opposition to commercial fur was focused on the terrible cruelty inflicted by the steel leg-hold trap, in which an individual animal may be in frightful pain for days before being killed. Since this could be denied neither by the trade nor its political and bureaucratic defenders, government funding was dedicated to the development of a "humane" trap. The "humane" trap study program necessarily involved animal experimentation. A varied succession of Mengelean fancies included drowning, strangling, crushing, clamping, and suffocating of captive individual mink, beaver, muskrat, red fox, bobcat, and others, by a variety of ingenious methods. The length of time it took for the animals to die was duly recorded. Sundry sorts of grisly traps and snares were prepared in both indoor and outdoor pens for captive martens, mink, fishers, lynx, and raccoons. The animals' agonized struggles were videotaped for detached scientific perusal.[17] Now it is generally acknowledged, even by many who used to be among its most fervent advocates, that "humane trapping" just might be a contradiction in terms.

The ultimate fall-back position of commercial fur interests has always been "ranched" (captive-raised) fur. Animals are not removed from the wild; therefore, there is no conservation issue. Animals are not trapped; therefore, there is no "humane" issue. The word "ranch" has attractive imagery about it. The (wild, not tame or domesticated) animals are reared in small wire cages, then killed ("harvested") by oral/anal electrocution, which does not damage the fur.

It took the industry some time to understand why those who would put down the trade[18] have been consistently unmoved and unimpressed by the "ranch" argument. What bothers the animal defenders, of course, is not only the patent cruelty of the animals' confinement and death, but also the commerce in parts and pieces of once-living, sentient, animate beings. Although they are primarily concerned with how the fur was obtained and the degree of animal suffering involved, they cannot comprehend the psychological orientation either of those who deliver the raw material or of those who would purchase the finished product. The latter are becoming conspicuously fewer.

The mythic insulation of commercial fur having been dissolved, the industry is gradually revealed for what it is — a strange and bizarre legacy of the exotic ideology of "resource" imperialism. The Canadian psyche is to a considerable extent constructed by historians out of the imagery of raw resource extraction, as part of a frontier mythology which is itself an expression of zero-order humanism.

I have devoted this chapter to two aspects of the role of Nature in subsidizing the human program — in science and technology, with medical research as an example, and in commerce, by way of the fur industry. The reader may or may not share my dubiousness about the medical establishment, but will surely have some unease about the fashion fur trade. Space does not allow me to discuss the use of living non-human beings in the testing of cosmetics and similar trivialities, products which I should think most sensitive people would consider something less than imperative.[19]

The role of Nature in the necessary subsidization of the human interest comes into sharpest focus in the use of animals for entertainment. Animals of all sorts, both wild and domesticated, are pressed into service for this purpose. Captive wild animals, whether "tamed," "trained," or incarcerated, are common currency in zoos, menageries, circuses, and side-shows. Free wild animals are for recreational killing, by way of either "hobby trapping" (a new, government-encouraged leisure activity, in Ontario at least) or "sport" gunning (long the life-blood of vested interests in "resource" bureaucracies). Domesticated animals entertain us as pets,[20] as performers in side-shows and competitions, and as adversaries in ritualized "conquest of Nature" re-enactments such as bullfights and rodeos.

There is a common quality about all this that makes one decidedly uncomfortable. It is not easy to identify. Setting aside for the moment the matter of physical and psychological cruelty, which is endemic and chronic, and the moral considerations, which are obvious, there remain in the Nature-as-entertainment phenomenon a number of much less clear-cut issues.

First of all, why is this form of human recreation so popular? It is easy to say that we enjoy seeing animals simply because they are beautiful, or grotesque, or different, or in some other way intriguing. Or, since they are not usually our daily urban experience, it is a refreshing change of pace. The very diversity of animal forms is fascinating. All this could well be the case with zoos, perhaps with special emphasis on the large "story-book" animals.

In my view, zoos convey and reinforce not only the "us" and (undifferentiated) "them" bifurcation of the living world, but also contrive to feed and nourish the fundamentalist myth of absolute human power and control. There are hard lines of glass or steel or moat between ourselves and "them," and we observe them at our pleasure. We keep them at a distance, and the psychological distance is quite as important as the physical. We *use* the animals, as we do any other devices, in the interest of our abstract, objective curiosity and possible edification. That is what zoos, and the animals in them, are *for*.[21]

Even more interesting, at least for this argument, is the merriment so often engendered by zoo animals. Imprisoned beings often develop bizarre and complicated tics. These are amusing. Any animal may at times do something to touch our funnybones — as often as not, something that may be anthropomorphically construed as vulgar —but the human mirth at any zoo is usually concentrated around the primates. Why do we so consistently laugh at the behaviour of non-human primates? The accepted explanation, which is valid at least in part, is that the monkeys and apes are seen as caricatures of ourselves. But where caricatures are often pointed and acerbic, these are more like comic strip or television cartoons. They are *silly*. The animals are "almost human" — but not really. They sometimes *look* as though they are almost human, but all of us know better. It is as though they are in some pathetic way *trying* to be human — trying to bridge the qualitative chasm that separates "us" and "them," the evolutionary gentry and the evolutionary peasantry. Their attempts are funny. To my ear, sometimes the laughter sounds ever so slightly hollow. No doubt it was also thus in another time, when people used to visit lunatic asylums for amusement.

Many zoos like to promote themselves as serious institutions of research, conservation, and education. Some do some of these things in greater or lesser degree, but all are in the business of entertainment. Many marine establishments are primarily side-shows, secondarily exhibits or aquaria. And there are those that are purely and simply amusement parks. Of these, the most interesting are those featuring animal performances very much like those of circuses.

A dolphin or a sea lion wearing a comic hat and sunglasses prompts much laughter. A macaw or a cockatoo or a bear riding a tricycle or struggling on roller-skates prompts more. I have seen film of "rock groups" consisting of chimpanzees, and of ducks. And of course there is the standard chimpanzee "tea party." Such items seem to have in common an incongruity, or absurdity, which is known to be a critical element in comedy.

In animal shows, the comedy is enhanced by the sheer *ineptness* of the performers. I have already indicated that it is a common ploy of zero-order humanism to judge animals by human standards in order to find them wanting. No one compares human athleticism with the standard set by a gibbon or a deer or a salmon, or human sensory perception with that of a homing pigeon or a lynx, or human social behaviour with that of a gorilla or a humpback whale. The game must be rigged unidirectionally, because the latter examples are not funny.

Also less than amusing is the operant conditioning to which the animals are subjected in the course of their "training." All good dog instructors know that the shortest and fastest route to the desired goal is positive reinforcement,[22] but such is not the case for side-show animals. The physical and psychological trauma captive wild animals endure in the course of developing the desired conditioned reflexes is not pleasant to contemplate. One must conclude that the patent cruelty involved is deemed necessary.

A final example of manipulative cruelty to animals in the interest of entertainment concerns the celebrated redneck institution of rodeo. Although rodeo is a competition between the human participants, the events are also between men (overwhelmingly) and animals. The animals are domesticated horses and cattle. Events purport to be illustrative of the traditional work of cowboys, but they would be more accurately described as the romantic cowboy mythology that persists in our society thanks to movies and television. Rodeo is very hard on animals.

All of the events in rodeo save one are based on the violent subjugation of domesticated animals. The exception is the "chuckwagon" race, in which horses are routinely killed in crashes.[23] The other events include the roping and tying of calves and steers, and the riding of bucking horses and bulls. I have seen no account of bull riding ever having been required in the good old days, and it is difficult to imagine what purpose was served by steer wrestling at home on the range.

I once had the good fortune to attend the rodeo in Cheyenne, Wyoming (one of the two top-ranking annual shows; the other is the Calgary Stampede), in the company of Elizabeth Atwood Lawrence and her husband. Lawrence, author of *Rodeo*, is a veterinarian and cultural anthropologist, with primary interest in the human–animal relationship. Her insights into what was happening to the animals and why were enormously instructive.

I saw a little Hereford calf killed outright as it ran at full speed, then was jerked high into the air as the noose around its neck was suddenly tightened by the weight of a big, strong horse. I saw a steer felled to the ground with a noose tightly wound around its head, pressing deeply into one eyeball. I saw much riding of bucking horses and bulls, and was surprised to notice that the bucking stopped the moment the event was over, and that the animals did not buck at all while in the "chute" where the riders mount them.

Then I learned about the flank strap. This device encircles the animal's body just in front of its hind legs. It is drawn tight at the instant the chute opens, and is released by an outrider the instant the rider dismounts or is thrown. Some say it irritates the tender skin near the animal's genitals, causing it to buck. Rodeo people deny this flatly, saying that it merely provides a little extra fillip to the animal's inherent jumpiness. Perhaps if it does not irritate the animals on its own, then bucking is a reflex to which they have been conditioned by the presence of the strap. I do know that neither horses nor bulls bucked without it.

There is more to rodeo, however, than even money,[24] cruelty, and *machismo*. It is clearly symbolic of a mythological structure.

On its deepest level, rodeo is essentially a ritual addressing itself to the dilemma of man's place in nature, exploring the boundary lines between people and other forms of life. It deals with the major theme of human supremacy over nature, and specifically with man's relationship to the animals which he conceives of as existing both within and beyond his sphere of control.[25]

Lawrence says that rodeo expounds a theme not only of the conquest of Nature, but also of that conquest as an *imperative*. This is clear in the performances. As well, however, Lawrence sees a sort of ambivalence about it all. It is necessary to conquer Nature, but at the same time it is necessary to leave some residue to conquer in future. The cowboy needs the wild in order to demonstrate his ability to subdue it. He needs a savage enemy through whom to show his strength and toughness.

This "commercialized brutality," as James Serpell calls it, is vigorously marketed to the ticket-buying public. In spite of the unconscionable cruelty involved, rodeo is presented as "harmless, red-blooded entertainment in which the cowboy — the epitome of wholesome manly virtue — uses his courage and skill to overcome and subdue untameable, outlaw stock. Doubtless the Romans employed similar fantasies to justify their activities in the Circus Maximus."[26]

As the seemingly infinite acts of violence in Cheyenne unfolded (there were many competitors in each event) I came to see the show as a sort of "one-note" morality myth — man defeats Nature — repeated, over and over and over again, endlessly and interminably, and without the slightest variation. Each repetition requires the use of a non-human "prop" to stand in the role of Nature. Many of the non-human animals are subjected to the same abuse several times daily. Wildness is simulated by domesticated animals bullied, goaded, and terrified into frantic resistance to the human performers. Thus is the myth maintained and reinforced. It must be perpetuated, because no more wildness would mean no more cowboy, no more heroic symbol of the primacy of the human enterprise. The flank strap is *necessary*.

157

For the reader who may feel that I have carefully selected extreme illustrations of zero-order humanism in order to make this argument, I should emphasize that the examples I have drawn from the fashion, research, and entertainment industries are typical. One could have made the identical point by way of such anomalous activities as recreational ("sport"!) killing, the puppy-mill business, the marketing of wild animal pieces and organs for quack medicine, the trade in "exotic pets," industrial (assembly-line) food animal production, feed-lot husbandry, standard and (especially) kosher animal slaughter, or indeed horse racing. None of these is unique. All share the common denominator of the human necessity. As human wants are so readily translated into human needs, so the assumed primacy of the human necessity is translated into the absolute human *right*.

ΠATURAL
RIGHTS

As we have seen, the human prosthetic device — the ideological surrogate for the natural wildness amputated in our self-domestication — deals in self-evident, manifest truths. From time to time, should such a truth require defence, we are entirely comfortable with rationalization, or as both R.D. Laing and Arthur Koestler, among many others, have pointed out, self-deception. At bottom, the prosthesis is, after all, about how-to-do-it, and rationality is its instrument. Many critics are wont to attack "instrumental rationality." There may be good grounds for suspecting that the instrumental sort is the only (or most dominant) rationality there is. When it fails to meet a particular challenge, reason automatically defaults back into the protection of chauvinist absolutism.

There is no other way in which to comprehend the zero-order orthodoxy of the absolute human right over Nature. If non-human beings are seen as useful to the human enterprise, it is right, fitting, and proper that they be so used. It is not easy to discern the necessity of animal use in commercial enterprises such as fashion, entertainment, and recreation; presumably that is subsumed by the greater purpose of commerce. As I have pointed out, legislation regarding cruelty to animals in biomedical and other research usually hinges on the presence or absence of necessity, but the definition is never made explicit.

The human necessity need not be spelled out because it is morally self-justifying and apparent, the ultimate trump card. It is widely seen as unseemly to search for the logical authority of any manifest truth. Such phenomena do not have roots; they are *givens*. They are in the rule-book from which all else proceeds. To question the rule-book is to devalue ideology itself. What makes this intolerable is the understanding that the only alternative to ideology is a chaotic, unpredictable, uncontrollable state of wildness. Ideology, as an insulating mythic structure, shields us from the reality of our own evolved biologic status in Nature. Within our protective stockade we cower in fear and dread of Nature and that which it implies. All despots have bunkers. Ours is zero-order humanism.

From the security of their bunkers, it is in the nature of despots to lash out. I have thought about these matters for a very long time, and the "siege mentality" metaphor seems best to fit the otherwise inexplicable fury with which it is the custom of the priests of human chauvinism to attack gentle folk such as, for example, "animal rights" advocates. There is no other way to explain the harsh intensity of the diatribes mounted against them, by "resource" managers and extractors and their political servants and by pillars of the "cultural" establishment and their sycophants.

The concept of animal rights is not easy to grasp, but this has not kept it from becoming contentious. Nor has it kept it from being invoked in context of the sorts of concerns outlined in the preceding chapter. It appears to be the inevitable fate of any once-useful term to become sloganized in the homogenizing digestive tract of the popular media. "Animal rights" (much like "environment" and "ecology") is now a code that is more symbolic than useful, bereft of most of its original meaning, but still convenient for those whose daily task it is not to produce thoughts but to fill space.[1]

The version of "animal rights" I shall offer here is somewhat at odds with that of many who are actively working in the field. I find "rights" a much more slippery notion than it would appear to be on the basis of its application. I am not at all persuaded of its value as a weapon with which to attack zero-order humanism. "Animal rights" has become a catch-phrase with profoundly negative connotations. More important is its apparent unsustainability as a concept. Not as a goal, or even as a policy, but as an *idea*.

Everyone who enjoys the close and constant company of non-human beings knows that there are certain reciprocal expectations involved. My wife and I observe "natural" fairness and justice in dealing with our dogs, and we expect "natural" decency and propriety from them. The dogs observe proper and reasonable social compliance in dealing with us, and clearly expect to be treated similarly. None of us is disappointed. For the most part we all do what is expected of us, and we do it without either coercion or conscience. One need not invoke rights, it seems to me, when a relationship rests on mutual trust, respect, and (especially) affection. Even though we are both the products of domestication, it is in the genetic inheritance of both dogs and people to be cooperative and mutually compliant in the shared social (family-centred) interest.

It is also in the genetic tradition of dogs and people to be ritualistic. Ritual plays a vital role in maintaining and reinforcing social bonds and family cohesion. Although such observances are customarily labelled "behaviours" by those who "work on" canids and primates, they are rituals all the same. Whether they involve preparation for the chase or for mating, or declaration of location or group identity, they are essential to continuity and stability in the social organization. Rituals are of the most fundamental importance.

Take for example dog walking. There are certain dark early mornings when sleet or freezing rain can make the ritual walk something less than appealing to both human and canid participants, but it is in the nature of ritual that it *must* be observed. It may be abbreviated, to be sure, but at the very least we must go through the motions. It avails the human Livingstons nothing to hope that the dogs will take a walk on their own, because they will not. Rather they will stand and call for us. They are both big, burly, self-confident individuals with nothing whatever to fear on their home ground, but they will not leave the immediate area of the house without either my wife or myself (preferably Ursula). In the morning, that is. During the rest of the day they do their independent "thing," but in the early morning the collective (group participatory) ritual must be observed without deviation.

It is pointless, indeed wrongheaded, to attempt to apply any fabricated structure of rights and duties, or claims and obligations, to an interspecies relationship of this sort. It has nothing to do with politics. Rather it is a manifestation of the family "self" which is available for access as the occasion requires. Ritual bond reinforcement is such an occasion. To suggest that the dogs have the right to demand our company, and we have the duty to provide it, is to perceive our relationship as a political one based on power and dominance, submission and subservience, tempered by an abstract system of moral canons. Such indeed is the prosthetic intrahuman condition, but such crippling of participatory consciousness does not prevail in Nature. It is true that the dogs are domesticated, as we are, but it is also true that they are not human. They are not the creatures of ideology.

Dogs tend to do the "right" thing most of the time because in

their social behaviour they enjoy the inherent "compulsion to comply." Within the immediate family and among close friends we do
the "right" thing most of the time because we share in that inheritance. In wider human affairs, however, we tend to do the "right"
thing as the result of abstract reflection. We weigh the situation,
and the cultural licences and taboos appropriate to it. Much of
our behaviour is governed by a construct of political ideas that has
been substituted for the genetic compulsion to comply. We were
forced to create a formal surrogate for compliance when human
social organizations became power-based. Anomalous (even pathological) in Nature, hierarchical dominance is the human norm.

The concept of "rights" arises from perceived inequalities and
inequities in the distribution of power and privilege in human societies. Like so many of our aberrations, the problem of access to
power is uniquely human. Both military coups and democratic
process are matters of the acquisition or the redistribution of power.
Power and privilege seen by those without them to be improperly or unfairly held or exercised invite a variety of responses ranging from criticism to violence. This creates the political and
intellectual environment for a concept of "rights."

A right is more than a legal claim subject to enforcement. There
is nothing moral or ethical about that; when some item is agreed
upon in a union–management negotiation, it may be seen by one
party as a rightful (meaning legal) claim upon the other only for
the duration of the contract. Other kinds of claims have longer
lifetimes, but always remain subject to modification and even cancellation through the political process. Most of our assumed dues,
however, do not appear in legal codes. Many are expressed in
resounding but very general terms in constitutions, charters, and
declarations for subsequent judicial interpretation, given the political mood of the day. Many more we create as we go along, according to the dictates of particular situations in which we find ourselves.

Some of the most elegant casuistry of which the rationalizing being is capable emerges in the public debate over human abortion. Here, "rights" are flung about not as concepts or ideals but as bargaining chips — even as tactical pre-emptive weapons. New rights emerge with the magical suddenness of mushrooms on a damp lawn. Virtually every rhetorical flourish from advocates representing all sides of the issue reveals some new absolute, some new and hitherto overlooked property of natural justice. In Canada, we have recently been instructed not only on the rights (claims) of foetuses against the women who carry them, and by extension against society, but also on the rights (claims) of former boyfriends to prevent women from obtaining abortions. Consistent with the ideology of zero-order humanism, however, the "right to life" is not applied to Nature.

Rights (usually no more carefully delineated than in the abortion debate) are employed by advocates for Native people in Canada in their struggle for release from generations of poverty and marginalization.[2] That their cause is just, and urgent, is indisputable. The white majority, however, by and large interprets Native "rights" as Native "claims." What is going to be claimed? How may it affect *me*? What right do these people have to make claims upon me? The possible permutations are endless. One derives the impression from recent events that Native people may have begun to talk a little less about abstract "rights," saving their breath for more concrete action.

Rights (however defined) are always transferred through concrete action. Once power and privilege have changed hands or been redistributed, it no longer matters what nuances of language or scholarship have been employed. Rights are willingly conveyed by or forcibly extracted from those who hold power. In spite of the legal scholars and philosophers, there is no such animal as a "natural right." One need only listen to Nelson Mandela to know what rights are made of. Rights are legal and political tools.[3]

Power and politics and rights and duties are necessary human concoctions in order that our societies, twisted and deformed though they are, may function in some reasonable semblance of order and peacefulness. We know in our tissue and bone and viscera that order and peacefulness are good, and natural, and that their absence is neither. We know that not as academicians but as biological beings. It is that inherent knowledge that prompts us to construct legal, moral, and ethical systems. It is usual to credit such constructions to "innate human decency." I believe it to be, rather, our vestigial inherent animal compulsion to comply.

If the concept of rights is, as I believe it to be, one of the "field marks" or symptoms, among many others, of human social pathology, then one might properly ask how it could possibly be of value in respect to beings who are free, wild, and whole. How could a domesticated human invention for domesticated human purposes be applied to the welfare of non-human beings?

It is important that we clearly distinguish between the motives of the animal rights advocates and some of their methods. Their motives are simple enough: empathy for living beings of sentience and sensibility, wrath at their maltreatment. There is nothing in the least puzzling about that; the activities of animal rights advocates are fuelled in equal measure by two of the most powerful of human emotions — compassion and anger. Having in mind the ridicule and aggressive denunciation they frequently encounter, to my certain knowledge they are singularly dedicated and courageous people. But I believe they have made themselves needlessly vulnerable.

The animal rights movement is vulnerable to criticism because of the inescapable implications of the fundamental concept of rights, which itself would appear to be (at best) inappropriate in the non-human context. Let us briefly review the arguments. They have been put forward by many people in many forms,[4] but the work of two scholars in particular has led the way.

165

The Australian philosopher Peter Singer, although he is generally regarded as the "father" of the animal rights movement, does not in fact address rights to any extent. His original popular vehicle was animal "liberation,"[5] which has quite different implications. The liberation of animals would be a conscious and unilateral act on the part of humans. It would not require the perception of "rights" inhering in animals; it would arise from the evaluation of human behaviour, wherever and however directed. This would not need to rest on the awarding to non-human beings of political status, or even of moral concern, but would be a simple recognition of the biological anomalousness of human interspecies actions.

Singer systematically disposes of traditional "deviousness" in such egalitarian philosophic positions as the "intrinsic" dignity and worth of the human individual, which, as every observer of our activities well knows, do not stand up even in intrahuman affairs. Conventional philosophy's further use in maintaining the human/non-human moral separation he finds "outrageous," calling our attention to "the ease with which not only ordinary people, but also those most skilled in moral reasoning, can fall victim to a prevailing ideology."[6] The essence of his position, which rests not on animal rights but on human ideology, is that "to discriminate against beings solely on account of their species is a form of prejudice, immoral and indefensible in the same way that discrimination on the basis of race is immoral and indefensible."[7]

Singer has few illusions, however, about the likelihood of human behavioural shift on grounds so ephemeral and elusive as goodwill: "I do not think that an appeal to sympathy and good-heartedness alone will convince most people of the wrongness of speciesism. Even where other human beings are concerned, people are surprisingly good at limiting their sympathies to those of their own nation or race."[8] But he does feel that most people are "at least nominally" prepared to listen to reason, and he devotes

166

his book to that audience, presenting an entirely cogent and reasonable case without recourse to any element which might be shown by even his most steadfast opponent as extreme.

Throughout this book I have relied on rational argument. Unless you can refute the central argument of this book, you must now recognize that speciesism is wrong, and this means that, if you take morality seriously, you must try to eliminate speciesist practices from your own life, and oppose them elsewhere. Otherwise no basis remains from which you can, without hypocrisy, criticize racism or sexism.[9]

Bernard Rollin, an American philosopher, addresses rights directly, and forcefully argues his case within the formal ground-rules of philosophic discourse. Since, in our society at least, rights are intimately interwoven with legal precedent and custom, Rollin begins there. Our legal systems are

inextricably tied to a set of moral principles that guide, constrain, limit, and influence the explicit laws that are adopted. So it follows that moral principles can and do serve as grounds of legal rights and obligations in the same way that explicit legal rules do.... [A]t the base of the legal system is the notion of moral rights possessed by persons. These moral rights follow directly from our recognition of persons as direct objects of moral concern, as entities worthy of moral consideration, as loci of intrinsic value, or, in Kant's terminology, as ends in themselves.[10]

Rollin argues that once we are able to see and accept persons as ends in themselves, then we recognize that there are aspects of their nature, their being, their *telos*, that must be protected. And they must be protected even against the greater general interest. (This is, of course, a purely human construct; tension between the individ-

ual and the collective has no meaning in Nature.) Literally, *telos*
means "end," or "completion." Rollin attractively adverts to the
telos of a spider, for example, being its nature and its function, its
gamut of activities intrinsic to it (he does not stoop to the economistic concept of "niche"), determined by evolutionary process and
genetic inheritance. Together, these elements add up to its "living
spiderness."[11] Spider as being, spider as end in itself. And not spider as species or some wider taxonomic unit, but spider as individual.

Rollin says, "The notion of rights is based on the basic moral
idea that ultimately the *individual* is the fundamental object of moral
concern and attention, that the individual has intrinsic value, and
that there are certain interests that are inseparable from his being
and, hence, themselves have intrinsic value."[12] Essentially, Rollin's
agenda, and that of the animal rights movement generally, is the
extension of moral concern for its *telos* to the individual non-human
being. One can have no quarrel with this on any intellectual or moral
grounds, but in our cultural ideology, non-human animals are not
beings but chattels. Even wild, free, non-domesticated animals in a
state of Nature "belong to the public." Once upon a time women
and slaves were chattels, and that was changed. With those and other
precedents in mind, our present task is to move non-human beings
into the arena of legitimate moral concern.

Once non-human beings have been shown to have a proper
claim to moral concern, then — and only then — would it be logical that legal rights be extended to them. In pointing out that both
our legal and our moral *Gestalt* on animals must change, however, Rollin sagely observes that "in part, changing the legal gestalt
will lead to new moral perceptions."[13]

To grant legal rights to animals is to institutionalize their
claim to moral concern, to recognize this status in a way

*that is writ large, to force us to pause and look at what we
take for granted and to confront the inexpedient and both-
ersome consequences of being moral agents. Certainly the
utilitarian costs are enormous, but so too were the opportunity costs of abolishing slavery and child labor.*[14]

I have quoted Bernard Rollin freely here, but would urge the
reader to refer to his books directly.[15] No one, in my view, has better, or more cogently presented the case for and against animal
rights within the accepted ground-rules of moral philosophy. Like
Peter Singer, he is coolly rational, without the slightest hint of
hyperbole or hysteria, and always scrupulously scholarly. I include
this comment because I have heard both philosophers portrayed
by vested interests in animal abuse as raving, roaring lunatics.

This is, in a manner of speaking, trump-card waving. Over twenty years ago the legal scholar Christopher Stone wrote an article[16]
which became a touchstone in natural philosophy. Stone asked "Should
trees have standing?" in exploring the possibility of the establishment
of legal standing — legal rights — for "natural" (non-human) objects.
One aspect of his discussion is especially useful: "Throughout legal
history, each successive extension of rights to some new entity has
been... a bit unthinkable.... The fact is, that each time there is a movement to confer rights onto some new 'entity', the proposal is bound
to sound odd or frightening or laughable."[17]

Laughter is a device much used by vested interests in the status
quo in any establishment. Laughter trivializes. Laughter and triv-
ialization, requiring no explanation or defence, are much used by
agencies of governments and by the animal-exploitive industries,
and widely purveyed by the steadfastly uncritical mass media. All
one need do to discredit any group advocating animal welfare is
label that group as consisting of "animal rights activists." Everyone
knows that animal "rights" are unthinkable. Ergo, by definition,
supporters of such a zany notion are loonies, crazies, and goof-

balls, and may be discounted.

The next step is to attach the "animal rights activist" label to *anyone* who is working in wildlife preservation or some other aspect of animal protection. The word "activist" is used indiscriminately. It is applied equally to those who have invaded experimental laboratories to liberate individual animal victims and to those such as Singer and Rollin whose labours tend to be almost exclusively cerebral. The phrase "animal rights activist" as unrelentingly purveyed by the media and by the animal abuse industries hinges for its effectiveness on the setting aside of differentiation. The biologist whose careful research shows that seals are not a threat to codfish is an "animal rights activist" because he happens to be talking about seals, and sealing is a hotly debated animal welfare issue. Thus he may be dismissed. The biologist who shows that trophy hunting is damaging the gene pool of some species of large mammal may be labelled an "animal rights activist" because he may be construed as being opposed to recreational killing. The biologist who shows on solid grounds that wolf-extermination programs are ecologically insane is also an "animal rights activist," and dismissable. Even those who seek to accomplish enforcement of the minimal laboratory anti-cruelty standards already on the books may be trivialized in this way. As Stone has put it, such interventions are unthinkable — odd, frightening, and (conveniently) laughable.

In the practice of the advocacy of non-human interests, "animal rights" is no longer an interesting concept but a pejorative. This is a critically important difficulty for those who would begin to dismember zero-order humanism. For them, time and energies are tightly budgeted, and their opposition is monumental, obdurate, and culturally entrenched. It would seem the better part of valour to resort to methods which have some greater apparent chance of success.

That discretionary comment is made not merely because rights for the non-human are ideologically unthinkable, but also — and of much greater importance — because the fundamental concept of rights seems itself to be incongruous and inappropriate in the non-human context. At its very simplest level, if the function of rights is political (to protect the interest of the individual against the interest of the collective), in whole, non-prosthetic Nature the notion is without meaning and, in Stone's terms, unthinkable. If, however, the function of rights is to protect Nature from humans, then that is to politicize Nature.

I have become persuaded that, in spite of my admiration for the quality and the rigour of the arguments that have been mounted on behalf of animal rights by philosophers and legal scholars, none is fully defensible. In order for animal rights arguments to be "rational" they must proceed from the starting-point of the established structure of Western ethical systems: "Western ethics are... human-chauvinist in that they characteristically take humans (or, to make a slight improvement, persons) to be the only items worthy of proper moral consideration, and sanction or even enjoin substantially inferior treatment for the class of non-human preference-having creatures, without — so it certainly appears — adequate justification."[18]

In practice, human moral and ethical constructs are used as the primary base on which most conventional cases for animal rights are built. If we are so much as to use the *language* of ethics, then we are bound to contain our arguments within the domesticated metaphysical dome of zero-order humanism. Conventional argument can take us no further than the power-based human political structure of interests and obligations, rights and duties, and the primacy of the individual. This is simply not good enough for Nature, for as I have attempted to show, Nature does not appear to be organized along the sociopathological lines of hierarchical dominance, and thus requires no form of antidote. Nature is of other stuff. It is wild.

Wildness is not acquired through covenant or dispensation. Wildness *is*, and has been, from the beginning. It is not merely an evolved phenomenon; it is a quality of being, and a precondition of having become. As such, it is beyond the reach of rationality; it is *previous*, and transcendent. It has no missing parts, either through mutation or amputation. It requires no prosthetic devices, no fixing, no reordering, no moral overlays. Wildness requires no organizational intervention, even of the purest and highest democratic sort. Wildness is whole. It is the antithesis of the domesticated human state, uncontaminated by power, claims to power, or the need for power.

There are, of course, multitudes of non-human beings who find themselves directly or indirectly in the power of humans, and subject to human whim. Non-human domesticates are among these, as well as individuals of wild species held captive. Although the latter are psychologically wild, they are not free to go; they have been subsumed into the human power apparatus. Whether kept as sources of human food, or for their skins and other body parts, as experimental laboratory inventory, or as entertainment commodities, these non-human beings have become part of our society, and thus of our political organization. Since rights were invented to protect the individual interest against the collective interest, it may be argued that rights would logically and necessarily apply to these non-human full-time participants in the collective enterprise.

I have discussed this matter at length elsewhere,[19] and will not develop that case in detail here. It will be sufficient to note that elements of Nature subject to our immediate whim and to our overt control are not necessarily under physical restraint or behind fences. There are for example those animals desired for recreational killing, or for their pelts; their interests, one might think, should be equally protected against those of the collective. They have no more choice in the matter of their relationship to humans than do their caged counterparts. As targets of our attention they too have been subsumed by our power apparatus. Logically, rights would apply.

Then there are those animals contained in national parks, nature and "game" reserves, many of which are so intensively managed as to be little more than extended menageries. Since it would be difficult to argue that captive zoo animals are not part of the human organization, presumably those of their kindred who happen to have a little more elbow room would similarly qualify.

Even in "wilderness" areas, non-human communities persist wholly at the human pleasure. A golden toad, a clawless otter, a pygmy hippo, a colobus monkey, a resplendent quetzal, each with its individual *telos*, is the total prisoner of the human decision to remove or not to remove its home. The free chimpanzee in its shrinking forest is no more immune to the human whim than its caged cousin in the AIDS laboratory. Even hitherto undisturbed natural places are locked into the hegemony of the human power structure.

If the idea of animal "rights" is to be taken seriously, then, it must be extended beyond the urban context, beyond agriculture, and beyond "resource management" to embrace the entire ecosphere and all of its individual non-human inhabitants. This may be an attractive notion at first blush, but even a modicum of thought reveals the most crashing irony. *It plays directly into the hands of zero-order humanism.* It represents the dedication of the entire planet to the human organization, the final conquest of Nature. The human power structure is total.

> *The ultimate question for the environmentalists* et al. *is whether all of non-human nature ought to move into the control of the human relationship. Presumably, the goal is to prevent such a relationship from developing. But, if it is prevented, then the goal of environmental rights must be*

*relinquished. Taken to its extreme, the result of the exten-
sion of rights would be to "humanize," or domesticate the
entire planet. All life would be a human farm.... [T]he price
of total conquest would be to confer rights on all species
concerned, usable against everyone. But past evidence of
the human conquest of nature displays massive extinctions,
widespread suffering and disfigurement. Accordingly, either
total domestication could not take place because each new
expansionist move would create a new array of rights to
stall it, or rights would have to be subtracted for a majority and selectively retained for a few. That would not amount
to moral or ethical behaviour toward those under our total
control as part of the planetary estate. The argument leads
to chasms of absurdity.*[20]

More recently, it has been put this way:

*The nub of the problem with granting or extending rights
to others, a problem which becomes pronounced when
nature is the intended beneficiary, is that it presupposes the
existence and the maintenance of a position of power from
which to do the granting. Granting rights to nature requires
bringing nature into our human system of legal and moral
rights, and this is still a (homocentric) system of hierarchy
and domination.*[21]

That system is the life's blood of zero-order humanism, as indeed
it is of any imperial structure. The "bottom line" continues to be
Caesar's thumb up or thumb down:

*To extend concepts of rights into nature — Caesar's ulti-
mate exercise of power — would be to export and legitimate a pathological obsession with hierarchical relationships.
As such, the choice is clear: either we must acknowledge the*

174

intrinsic "rightness" of non-human existences and sensibil-
ities and express that acknowledgement in human *behav-*
iour, backed by law, or, complete the "humanization" of
the planet by making all living things unwitting participants
in a prosthetic moral hierarchy.[22]

I should think that any naturalist would feel that wild non-human beings would just as soon go their own way and take their chances. One cannot imagine them willingly casting their lot with the chronically stressed and impoverished community of domesticates for whom rights had to be conceived in the first place. It is for these reasons that I conclude that "animal rights," if carried to its logical conclusion, is potentially destructive to the quality of wildness — the essence of untrammelled being. Rights must be seen and understood for what they are: artificially institutionalized technical surrogates for naturally evolved mutualistic, participatory compliance and reciprocity. Even in human affairs, rights are prostheses for "rightness."[23]

Insistence on "animal rights," no matter how pure or decent our motives, is insistence on the perpetuation of an artificial (political) construction of the nature of being. Worse, it is to draw all of non-human life into the bonds of crippling ideological subservience. It is to beg the root issue: that our cultural perspectives on Nature and our treatment of the non-human are not merely "wrong" in some contrived moral philosophic sense, but monstrous and unnatural.

SWEET
BONDAGE

Some of the material in the previous chapters may strike some readers as an indictment. That is not my intention. My aim in writing this book has been descriptive. Domestication, as a process and as a condition, is a very useful glass through which to understand the distanced, even alienated position the human species has adopted in its relationship to Nature. If my choice of words and images, and the examples I have used have at times seemed something other than objective, that is because my concern for living non-human Nature is entirely subjective and value-laden. I offer no apologies for that. As an organism of ordinary sensibility I do not know what it is to be objective.

At the conclusion of "Natural Rights," I observed that our cultural perspectives on Nature and our treatment of the non-human are monstrous and unnatural. That is not a moral judgment. It is a naturalist's interpretation of the phenomena that surround him.

I see in human interspecies behaviour a theatre of the grotesque, a pageant of the deviant. I see a being estranged from its roots and its natural context committing the most improbable and aberrant acts under the self-justification provided by its own obsessive narcissism. That is what I see.

I have hypothesized that the reason for our aberrant behaviour is that we evolved as a domesticated species. We show almost all of the features we have built into those other animals manufactured in our image and brought into our fold. To offset the crippling physical and psychological effects of their fabricated condition, and to enable them to function from day to day, and to survive long enough for us to kill them, such beings require a "prosthetic device" to stand in the place of that part of their naturalness — their wildness — that has been amputated. For them, the prosthesis is us, upon whom they are utterly dependent.[1] For us, the prosthesis is ideology, upon which we are similarly dependent.

Our dependence on ideology (abstracted systems of belief) arose out of our technical specialization, which is conceptual skill devoted to instrumental means. And it has been stressed that in spite of our physical destructiveness, the effects of which are everywhere apparent, much more important are the ideas that nourish and sustain the human project. As our dependence on rationalistic ideology deepened, there was (as in all species of domesticates) a concomitant loss of sensibility to our community context, to Nature. We evolved both biologically and culturally into ecological misfits with a fanatical dedication to the universal primacy of our enterprise. The goal, simply put, is the humanization of the entire planet, its remaking in our image — domesticated, predictable, and controllable.

This should not be read as a mere metaphor. It should be read as a surmise concerning the genesis and evolution of human interspecies destructiveness.[2] It should be received as a diagnosis.

Although it does not include a prescribed course of treatment, neither is it foreclosure or capitulation. If, as I have long conjectured, we — as a species — have a piece missing, and, as I have suggested here, that piece is culturally replaced by ideology, then it would seem to behoove us to address our ideologies. Not that we can do without them; we cannot. But we can most certainly do without some of our cultural impedimenta; both we and Nature could benefit from some drastic shuffling of received wisdom.

It is not my purpose here to offer either a cookbook or an agenda. I am deeply suspicious of "fixes," especially those presented as lists or tablets instructing us on the dos and don'ts, ins and outs, goods and evils, appropriates and inappropriates, whites and blacks, and most especially if they carry the tag "environmental."[3] This is not a matter of binary choice. It never has been, and never will be, because we are dealing with complex, often contradictory, always problematic, evolved and evolving phenomena. Cultures are never static. They are always moving and adjusting not only to the "main chance" of the moment but also in response to winds, currents, and shifting cargo. Such changes are slowed, sometimes, by accretions of barnacles, but these are, after all, susceptible to treatment. Hull-scraping is called for.

Just as ships' bottoms pick up layers of barnacles over time, so, through their lives, human societies and individuals become encrusted with layers of cultural and ideological sediment. When you suffer from encrustations, you cannot always remember where you picked them up, especially if you have exposed yourself to them repeatedly and over a period of time. At my age, for example, it is exceedingly difficult to identify with any confidence whatever when the first free-drifting particulates fetched up upon me, and took hold. My initial response to their presence, when I was eventually told of it, was the customary denial. How could I possibly be carrying accretions about with me? And, later, even if I am, what is wrong with that? These are *good* accretions. They are the accumulated wisdom of my culture, of all of time. (I forget that there was a period of time before my culture emerged.) These accretions are natural, and proper, like the callosities on the head of a right whale. Neither the whale nor I would be what we are without them. They are not disfiguring; they are *me*.

This is entirely accurate. But it is equally accurate to say that I would still exist without them. There is beneath the cemented debris of my cultural conditioning a live animal with most of the normal attributes of animalness. I carry within me a prosthetic implant, to be sure, but apart from that I am whole, and the prosthesis itself can be erased and reprogrammed. Should I contrive a way to free myself of them, potentially I will be in pretty good shape. It might even be liberating. So I decide to do just that — at least to whatever extent I am able. Since this is not a physical but an intellectual challenge, I shall simply have to think them away.

Thinking away the concreted residue of zero-order humanism is not easy, nor is it painless. The cemented coating clings as though chemically bonded to me, and it screams bloody murder at my slightest advance. But I am after all using my specialties, conceptualization and abstraction, in which, as a human being, I am uniquely gifted. It is what I *do*. It is how I evolved. So I do it. Not that one can become a *tabula rasa*, but neither would one want to. There is much that is good, and sensible, buried beneath the humanistic overlays.

Paul Shepard, in his powerful account of our arrested development, concludes with the positive reminder that "there is a secret person undamaged in every individual,"[4] and that "we have not lost, and cannot lose, the genuine impulse. It awaits only an authentic expression."[5] The impulse is latent in the child, but must be nourished and released through intimate experience, including bonding, with Nature. This is part of our evolved, human, being.

Shepard emphasizes that "civilized ways inconsistent with human maturity will themselves wither in a world where children move normally through their ontogeny."[6] Mature human individuation will produce cultural shift.

We will always, however, be domesticates; we will always require a prosthesis. We will always be governed by ideology. Shepard's model emphasizes that the bonding to Nature is essential to mature individuation, which in turn involves personal bonding to the cosmos, with the full spiritual development that implies. I interpret this, for my purposes, as confirming that, although we will always require ideology, it is the fullness and maturity of development of that ideology that counts.

There can be little doubt that we shall always specialize in "how to." That is in the very structure and function of the human brain. We are *the* technical animal. I must acknowledge here, however, that there are thoughtful people who say that "how to" is insufficient, and that to save ourselves and Nature we must shift into some different intellectual configuration altogether. "How to" dictates the way of viewing the world (objective, proprietary, utilitarian, manipulative, instrumental) that has ignited the global human holocaust. There must be an alternative way of human being in the world.

Finding that way, however, depends first on asking how. We are entirely capable of abstracting new ends, contriving new means. Assuming the will to do so (a critical and perhaps irresponsible assumption), we can at any time expunge the most blatantly destructive ideologies and beliefs from our cultural catalogue.

One useful place to begin might be the scientifically and popularly held idea that human and non-human social organizations must rest on dominance relationships. I have adverted already to the wrongheadedness of this queer dogma in both ecology and ethology, and the lamentable way in which it is used to rationalize human sociopathology, and to celebrate such anomalies as competitive individualism.

Anthropologists have observed that in human societies in which possessions are held in common, competition, dominance, aggression, and all the other manifestations of the invisible hand are unknown.[7] The psychological dimension is equally interesting.[8] Both indicate that competition is not innate in us, but learned. Both show that competition is by its very nature destructive. Both offer cooperation as its opposite, usually holding that the human species is the most cooperative of all primates. This, I feel, is unnecessary to the argument. There are simply more visible signs of human cooperation around us than there are from other primate species. If a species is cooperative, then it is cooperative.

In any case, cooperation may be seen as a second, narrower level of behaviour within the wider phenomenon of compliance. Species may be compliant without being overtly cooperative. The compliant model of natural reality which I have ventured to construct in this essay rests on the notion of "at-one-ship," a state of being which the naturalist is able to infer from the behaviour of wild non-human social groups and multispecies communities. In spite of persistent denial by the cultural prosthesis (we are "different"), human beings still share in that fundamental quality. Among domesticates, we are one of only two species to whom self-awareness beyond the individual appears to remain available.

Deep in the process of attempting to abstract away my ideological encrustations, hap'ly I think on the dog. I recall that the dog and I, unlike all other domesticated beings, are descended from ancestors who were cooperatively participatory in the interest of the family-centred social group. Neither of us has lost that quality. Both of us are prosthetic beings, to be sure, but unlike all others we clearly retain the compulsion to comply. Even more important, we retain it across our respective species boundaries.

Humans are accepted into the family of the dogs, they into ours.

In spite of the common currency, there is in my household no power structure and no dominance hierarchy, patriarchal or otherwise. There is a cooperative enterprise in which everyone does what is expected toward the common interest. My wife and I provide food and shelter, the dogs provide security, and interspecies communication and experience. All parties contribute to entertainment, play, and good fellowship. Both of our dogs (a Newfoundland and a St. Bernard) are stronger than I am, so there is no question of physical coercion. They have learned the words, and perhaps other signals for what is expected of them, and they do it. My wife and I have learned the signals for what the dogs want, and we do that.

Whether compliance can prevail beyond the family-centred group may depend on our appreciation of self-awareness as suggested in "Other Selves," and on the alternatives to economistic biological science offered in "The Exotic Ideology" and "Nature's Marketplace." To my certain knowledge, self-as-group occurs in other human contexts much wider than family — comradeship in arms, in team sports, in some common-interest alliances, and so forth. Self-as-community and self-as-biosphere are extensions in degree, not changes in kind. If the group consists of more than one species, as the dog–human relationship attests, then one is already experiencing compliance at about the community level. Self-as-biosphere, the transcendent or peak experience, is known by all of us. It may be infrequent or rare, but it is.

Similarly, I am satisfied that it is interspecies compliance that, in effect, maintains and sustains the complex interwoven fabric of natural communities and associations, and the integrity of regions and biomes. As I have argued earlier, competition could never achieve results so ineffably perfect, because competition is about rivalry, and striving. No horseshoe crab or bustard or buffalo of my acquaintance ever strove, so far as I can tell. But each complied, in living and dying, with the needs and requirements of its community, by the simplest and most beautiful of expedients — by being.

But the rogue primate has introduced an entirely new and unprecedented manner of being. With conceptual and technical skills the like of which have never before emerged on Earth, and with unequalled powers of abstraction, the problem animal has become enabled not only to consume or obliterate elements of non-human Nature at virtually its slightest whim, but also to rationalize that activity in comfortably self-reassuring terms. This is the function of zero-order humanism. The power of this ego-centred orthodoxy extends, however, even beyond its use as an instrument of self-deceiving justification. It constructs the world in which we function. The human mission to dominate becomes more than a mere historicist or determinist expression of our achievements; it becomes the evolved nature of things, the way the world is and was meant to be. It becomes an unassailable and incontrovertible "reality."

The "reality" upon which we customarily hang our mission to dominate is the concept of the future.[9] Obviously, all technical or instrumental thinking, and all "progress" orientation requires the prior assumption of goals, and the assumption of goals in turn necessitates the prior abstraction of the future. Forward-thinking by most animals appears to be confined to the duration of the task at hand — the strategy of the hunt, the best approach to the immediate challenge, the weighing of options in the here and now.

Non-human beings and a shrinking number of human societies have always lived in the joyous fullness of the present. Our society has contempt for their unwillingness to be victimized by morbid obsession with what may or may not happen tomorrow. The Western future-orientation is virtually total. Our self-identities as individuals and societies — maybe even as a species — appear to be cast in terms not of what we have been, not of what we are, but of what we shall *become*. But *only humans become*. Non-human beings may be seen as evidence of the creativity of evolution, but humankind must be seen differently. Our species must be seen as the culmination and realization of life's purpose. The future of planet Earth is the *human* future. All species are mortal, save only one.

Of course, the future never comes. Our self-identity is never found. Having long since abandoned our self-identity as *Nature*, we chose to put all our chips on the future, whose margin, like that of Tennyson's Ulysses, fades forever and forever as we move. No matter; the priests and the secular gurus, and the humanists generally, keep flogging it.

But if we identify solely with the future, then surely we never grow up. Paul Shepard's "arrested development" thesis[10] applies here. As individuals, societies, and civilizations, we are forever *becoming*, forever questing for mature adulthood. It follows that in the advancement of our quest whatever must be done, must be done. If it means the simplification and homogenization of natural communities and processes, so be it. If it means the extirpation of whole floras and faunas — without replacement —then that is in the nature of things.

The human enterprise is *necessary*. The human future is *imperative*. The subsidy Earth and earthly non-human beings are required to pay for human immortality is, of course, factored out, not in. That is an externality — an incalculable, as the technocrats like to say. Regrettable, perhaps, but necessary and inescapable.

This leads us to ask how the future, however outlined, is to be "sustained." The *idea* of the future we sustain by mantra, litany, catechism, ideology, and a good shot of group self-mesmerism — to say nothing of human-chauvinist narcissism. The *realization* of the future — the necessary advancement of the human monoculture — is to be sustained by Nature.

The clear assumption is that Nature *owes us*. It is Nature's appointed task — its reason for being — to maintain and nourish the human project. Nature was provided to serve the Chosen Species. That is the received cultural and historical wisdom that sustains such madnesses as "sustainable development."

Unfortunately, there is little reason to think that the human community is about to address the ideological content of the cultural prosthesis. Some of us chip around the edges, but most of us go about our business within the metaphysical enclosure of received realities. Those realities are unceasingly reinforced by science and technology, and, in their scientistic modes, by the arts and humanities, by social and political theory, by economics and commerce, and by popular knowledge of that which is manifestly true, self-evident, and natural. This is not a conspiracy, nor is it even a commonality of interests. It is a cosmological datum.

This is the primary reason why zero-order humanism is so rarely called upon to explain or justify itself. It is also the reason why most of those who would work to improve the lot of non-human Nature in the world customarily contain their arguments within the ground-rules of conventional human-centred discourse. Why *not* couch our case for Nature protection in terms of the human interest? Why flail at windmills when there are so many wrongs to be put right here and now, in our own backyards? Why try to blow up the entire human metaphysical dome when there is so much within it calling for immediate attention? Why not attempt to do what is possible, what *works*?

When one is very tired, or very discouraged, these can be attractive propositions. But they are not good enough. They are tame, obedient, subservient reflexes. In the Norwegian philosopher Arne Naess's terminology, they are "shallow";[11] in Bill Devall's, they are "reformist."[12] I call them domesticated. Familiar examples abound: resource management, resource conservation, sustainable development, environmental impact assessment, environmental planning, animal rights, much but not all green politics, and indeed "environmentalism"[13] itself. It is not even so much the inadequacy of such within-the-system tinkering that disturbs one (if you are working within the system, you are part of the problem); it is much more that silence on (and, indeed, avoidance of) the "root" issues may be taken as tacit endorsement of the zero-order imperative. This is not to deprecate what some environmentalism does, but to emphasize what it does not do. It may occasionally lighten the weight of the human hand on Nature, but it rarely redirects it and it never attempts to short the circuitry that runs it. Environmentalism never, ever, gets at the neural hypertrophy that the circuitry serves.

A case in point is the role of "the environment" in current politics. Quotation marks are used because the politicians never get around to telling us what, for their purposes, the word means. From their pronouncements, however, it is clear that "environment" means either resources or pollution sink, or both. This has a strikingly familiar ring: "environment" is the new label on the old wine bottle that used to be called "Nature," explicitly undefined but implicitly received as free material commodities and garbage commons.

Politicians tremble and quiver with intensity, excitement, and earnestness as they vie for recognition as the most passionate defenders of natural goodness. Political parties compete for pre-eminence in being "for the environment." How that odd expression is to be construed is studiously left open. What is not left to anyone's imagination, however, is where a given political ideology stands in respect to zero-order humanism. The "Greens" excepted, it is impossible to name a political gospel of whatever hue that does not celebrate resourcism and industrialization. Industrialization

186

of *any* sort is inevitably at the cost of wild Nature. There is no such thing as an "environmentally friendly" industrial-growth economy. Being "for the environment" means business as usual, with a careful eye to its sustained growth and development in safety and security.

All of us (certainly we professors) are accustomed to the unremitting din of fiery protest against "capitalism." What is meant, of course, is *private* capitalism; state capitalism tends to go unscathed. That the primary goal of both is industrial growth and development is usually ignored. On this ground at least, there is no distinction whatever between the poles of left and right. The necessary primacy of the human enterprise dominates both.

It may be that if a concern for Nature is ever to enter and become integrated within a political ideology, we should not expect it to happen within either of the old-line left/right streams. It will need to be something new altogether. "Reform" of traditional positions will be insufficient. Those parties that historically have single-mindedly served corporate and chamber of commerce interests cannot possibly unburden themselves of their nineteenth-century devil-take-the-hindmost resourcist orientation to the world. On the other hand, we have become quite used to hearing the left proclaim itself as environmentally sensitive and responsive in the most modern and enlightened sense. This too is questionable.

Robyn Eckersley, a political philosopher with a particular interest in the Green movement, has provided a fascinating analysis of the role of socialism in environmentalism. The method is novel: comparing and contrasting the philosophies of Karl Marx and John Muir, the American champion of wilderness preservation and founder of the Sierra Club. Eckersley points out that modern ecophilosophers

challenge the essentially human-centred *philosophical roots*

187

of Marxism in arguing for the intrinsic *value of nonhuman phenomena. Of the many strands of environmentalism, it is clearly the preservationist strand within the modern environmental movement that is the most foreign to mainstream Marxists, especially when couched in terms of "wilderness for its own sake" rather than for its instrumental value to us, i.e., as a means to human ends (say, for sport and recreation, aesthetic appreciation, science or raw materials for future generations)...*[14]

This is what Naess originally termed "shallow" environmentalism. Devall and others, perhaps because of the pejorative English connotations of "shallow," have tended to use "reformist" or some equivalent. Many Nature preservationists see it as "anthropocentrist." This invites attack from entrenched humanism.

The standard Left rebuff [to the preservationists] to the effect that Muir and his followers are misanthropic merely betrays the Left's narrow moral universe and outmoded picture of the human and nonhuman worlds as two mutually exclusive zones; it also explains the zeal with which the Left are prepared to pursue a road to social justice that wreaks havoc on the nonhuman world.[15]

Although not everyone would go as far as Eckersley does, there seems small doubt that modern post-Marxist democratic socialism, although perhaps a way-station on the road to a "Green ecotopia," is most certainly not yet there. Having in mind its radical, fundamental, and unswerving dedication to the human interest, it will not likely get there.

We may, however, have reason for hope in at least some aspects of the Green movement, which has been measurably influential in European and Australian politics if not yet in North America. George Sessions, who with Bill Devall originally introduced and argued Arne Naess's "deep ecology" on this continent, shows (following Naess) that there are within the Green movement three approaches: "(1) those solely concerned with human society, (2) those which combine society and Nature, and (3) those solely concerned with Nature."[16] There remains some division within the Green movement on which direction should be followed, or, if all three are followed, which should receive the greatest emphasis. Assuming that the Greens do penetrate North American politics in a significant way, a good deal will hinge on their internal policy decision. For those who know the term, "bioregionalism" appears to be an example of the second approach.

There is one especially interesting aspect of the current political landscape, and that is the matter of human populations. At one time a widely debated and much analysed problem of the day, human population pressure has mysteriously slipped from both political and popular "environmental" agendas. We still hear of it, of course,[17] and it is unfailingly mentioned in conservation and development strategies and along the industrial globalization network, but it does not attract the concentrated attention it once did. Nice people (and not only socialists) do not talk about such nasty things any more. There is plenty of talk about food distribution (there is food for everyone in the world if we could only get it to them) and both industrial and low-impact agriculture, but the matter of absolute human numbers appears to have receded, if not from our private reflections, from our public utterances.

The deadliest and most insidious form of thought repression is self-censorship. To inhibit the expression of one's own views and conclusions is the ultimate in self-domestication. It has become popular among adherents to "social ecology" (a term meaningless in itself, but apparently a brand of anarchism) to label those who would dare to weigh the interests of Nature in the context of human populations as "ecofascists." Yet another trump card. Charges of fascism and misanthropy, as well as of racism and Malthusianism, are familiar to all who tend the vineyards of Nature's inherent worth in the face of the human blight. The self-censorship that sometimes can follow, though craven and submissive, is usually defended as necessary and unavoidable pragmatism.

It was not always thus. There was a period in which a great deal of attention was given to exploding humanity. From the later 1940s to the early 1970s there was a formidable outpouring of articles and books[18] on the social and ecological implications of unrestrained human breeding. Most of this work was by ecologists, some by nutritionists and others, but all considered the danger real, and imminent. Retrospectively it is interesting to see the following in Bernard M. Baruch's 1948 introduction to William Vogt's *Road to Survival*:

> [This] is, I believe, the first attempt — or one of the first... to show man as part of his natural environment, what he is doing to that environment on a world scale, and what that environment is doing to him. It is no dry-as-dust study; it deals with the raw stuff of living, how more than two billion men and women and children — including you and me — are to be fed, and sheltered, and clothed, and whether or not they are to live in peace, tomorrow, and next year, and in the year 1975.[19]

By 1975 the world human population was no longer two thousand millions but four thousand millions. Baruch was not the only person to cast ahead to that year. In 1967 there appeared a book with the title *Famine — 1975!* by the brothers Paul and William Paddock, a diplomat and an agronomist, respectively. Both had worked for many years in the "undeveloped" world. Vogt's book had been among the first to look at the global human condition from an ecologic point of view; nineteen years later, the Paddocks' was the first to seriously argue for the use of *triage*[20] in international food assistance programs. The year 1975 came and went, as it developed, without the worldwide human catastrophe predicted. But not without famine, and not without the ignition of hot wars and the social dislocation of uncountable throngs of the oppressed and the dispossessed in the overpopulated, unproductive, soil-poor low latitudes. Since that time starvation and internal and international tensions and flare-ups have steadily increased in the tropics and subtropics precisely along the anticipated lines. The inexorable laying waste of Nature has broadened, deepened, and accelerated proportionately. The fact that the human population bubble has not yet burst in all of its horror does not mean that it will not. The fuse is no longer sputtering. It is burning steadily now. No organism can increase its numbers infinitely.

No doubt the familiar devices of distancing and denial are at work in the disappearance of the population question. It has seemed to me for quite some time that the continuing reportage of the Ethiopian and Somalian famines tends to focus on the human misery, the "failure" of the rains, and the bitterly drawn-out political violence. Little attention is given to the human role in the ecological synergy that causes desertification. Although much is made of the hideous suffering of the children, few commentators note that if there were such a thing as natural justice, these little ones would never have been. Even fewer address the ironical human ability to proliferate even under the most appalling privation. No wild animal can do that.

There are *machismo* tenets in some human cultures that must rigidly reject family planning no matter what the consequences. In others, repeated reproduction has become a perceived means of offsetting child mortality. There are others whose "leaders" are sufficiently chicken-hearted and sexist to deny women a choice in the matter of abortion. There are still others with "policy makers" bent on providing more customers for the chain stores, more victims for the financial institutions, and more non-corporate tax-payers by enhancing natural increase through immigration. There are even governments desirous of rapid population increase for purely political reasons. In all nations, rich and poor, there is una-nimity on the point that the effect of human numbers on Nature is a second-order consideration, an externality.

Anyone who knows anything about living organisms knows that the human reproductive wave is anomalous and unnatural. No other animal, especially a large one, could possibly get away with it. In Nature, explosions do occur at times, but either they are cyclic and normal, as with lemmings, or there is some unusu-al, local reason for them (more often than not traceable to human activity). In either case they tend to die back as suddenly as they arose. There is a variety of ways in which the lid is kept on local wild animal populations: diminishment of food supply, increased predation pressure, emigration, disease, and physiological and behavioural inhibition against breeding. In Nature, one or more of these restraints normally comes into play before a population gets seriously out of hand.

This is not the case with domesticates. Unlike most wild animals, they mate right around the calendar. They come to sexual maturity early in life, and they are sexually vigorous and promiscuous. They are wide-spectrum feeders and they can succeed in a diversity of habitats. They thrive in simplified and homogeneous circumstances, and they will tolerate a high degree of crowding. They have little or no cross-species or community sensibility. There are too few large natural predators left in the world to have any effect on their increase, and thanks to our ministrations they are generally fairly healthy. Even when they are not in good condition, however, they continue to reproduce. They have no physiological, behavioural, or ecologi-cal constraints on their fruitfulness. They are bred to breed.

In addition, the domesticated primate is bred to think. Many and varied have been the human individuals who have dared to engage the population dilemma and to express their thoughts publicly. Few have been so wild (undomesticated) in their forthrightness as Robert Heilbroner, who has had the intellectual and social courage to say, for example, that exploding child mortality by undernourishment in the poorest countries is "a human tragedy of immense proportions, but also a demographic safety valve of great importance."[21] This is merely an observation of how population dynamics actually work. Further,

these Malthusian checks will exert even stronger braking effects as burgeoning populations in the poor nations press ever harder against food supplies that cannot keep abreast of incessant doublings. At the same time, the fact that their population "control" is likely to be achieved in the next generations mainly by premature deaths rather than by the massive adoption of contraception or a rapid spontaneous decline in fertility brings an added "danger" to the demographic outlook. This is the danger that the Malthusian check will be offset by a large increase in food production, which will enable additional hundreds of millions to reach childbearing age.[22]

The rest of the scenario is familiar: intensified "miracle" crop production with Niagaras of inorganic pesticides, chemical fertilizers, and children, none of which limited non-temperate soils can sustain. Massive migration to the cities creates further environmental and social disarray. The terrible increase in the pressure of poverty, sickness, and sheer numbers indicates defensive entrenchment by the élites. Tinpot dictators soon follow, with wars virtually inevitable. The zero-order humanists notwithstanding, "Malthusian" is not a dirty word. It is shorthand for "the natural and inevitable effects of population pressure."

These sorts of predictions have become all too common (but no less valid for that), and I shall not pursue them further here. I am more concerned to make two points: first, the proliferation of all domesticated animals is subsidized by the simplification and homogenization, and ultimately the destruction, of natural communities; second, and even more important, in the case of the human domesticate, zero-order ideology holds that no price is too great to be demanded of Nature toward that subsidy. Human imperialism is both natural and necessary.

The human situation in the world is replete with ironies. The interests of Nature have never been part of the cost/benefit calculus of the human endeavour. Yet, paradoxically enough, it is our (prideful) cultural forswearing of our connections to Nature that has brought both us and Nature to our present pretty pass. Sheep and goats don't know any better; we are supposed to. We are inordinately proud of our systems of "values," for example, but we seem unable to translate those values into the reality of our living being, as co-inhabitants of an evolved and evolving community of myriad existences. A wise and gentle man by the name of Stan Rowe has put it this way:

In the crunch ... the Ecosphere (Nature) ought to be valued above people on the basis of precedence in time, evolutionary creativity and diversity and the complexity of a higher level of organization. Conceivably, for example, present human population, expanded in size by technology, has become an active evil, exceeding the sustainable limit, overwhelming the planetary environment. The ultimate crimes against the environment, crimes that also threaten the human enterprise, are fecundity and exploitive economic growth, both encouraged by the homocentric philosophy.[23]

"Evil" is a formidable word, but not an extreme one. If, after all, life diversity is manifestly good in an absolute sense, then its wanton spoilage and eradication is the opposite. Our behaviour is not just bad, or injurious, but since it occurs with full knowledge of its nature and consequences, and is even ideologically justified as necessary, it becomes something worse. The sacking and pillage of Nature is predetermined and with intent: biocide aforethought. This charge must not be attached to the starving multitudes who are, quite naturally, fully occupied in trying to stay alive. It is reserved rather for the timorous politicians, stricken immobile in fear of addressing population policy. It is reserved also for the fanatical ideologues of the realization of human purpose and meaning through planetary conquest. Most particularly and specifically guilty is the international commercial "development" enterprise which would domesticate all beautiful and wonderful things non-human into its own noxious image, and would see the process as natural, inevitable, and good.

You and I are accessories. We elect weak, self-serving politicians who, together with their devious, self-serving senior bureaucrats, assiduously evade the "crunch" issues of population and "development" policies, and whose only allegiance is to their jobs. We buy furniture made of tropical hardwood. We buy tuna fish at the "incidental" cost of hundreds of thousands of dolphin deaths. We buy shares in chemical companies. We do business with Japan, paramount despoiler of wild Nature. We allow recreational killing, and we condone the flaying of wild animals for fashion. We donate funds to vivisection. We allow our children and grandchildren to be brainwashed into the technical, technocratic, and managerial infrastructure of zero-order humanism.

That we, the educated, the informed, the well nourished, the affluent, do so pathetically little to stall the human juggernaut (consisting, after Rowe, of equal measures of fecundity, exploitive commercial growth, and anthropocentric belief systems) is testimony perhaps to our physical comfort, perhaps to our domesticated apathy, perhaps to our arrested ontogenies, perhaps to our evolved, intrinsic askewness.

Perhaps our failure to challenge zero-order humanism is a consequence of our servile thraldom to ideology itself. If that should indeed be the case, then there would be very little that we could do about it. We must have ideology in order to function in domestication. But as I have insisted throughout this essay, as biological beings we still have access to our own nature. That is a statement arising from an ideology different from the prevailing version. It is one that allows us first to understand and then to reject zero-order humanism together with all of its arrogant, cruel, and unnatural appendages. It allows us then to seek a structure of ideas and beliefs that will be built not on future (abstract) desires and expectations, but on past (experienced) qualities of active bonding and participation.

The experience of wildness. Like its close kin which we call freedom, wildness is perceptible only in its absence. Both are forever paradoxical. Percy Shelley saw freedom as "sweet bondage."[24] We may see wildness similarly: a state of being in which one is an autonomous organism, yet bonded and subsidiary to the greater whole. Of the miraculous, multitudinous life adventure, one is at once the end and the means, a unique expression and the totality. Self without boundaries is sweet enough, but oneself in a muskrat or a tamarack is sweeter still.

We all share in this. If every child has the "genuine impulse," then every adult can remember. For some of us, the experience of non-human Nature is the most vivid recollection of young childhood. Not the cognitive, but the affective experience. And certainly not the "wilderness" experience, because wilderness is a human abstraction only. I mean the dissolution of the ego-centred self, as when one was drawn close, ever closer and at last into the gold-flecked eye of a toad, or when one melted into black earthy humus, laced with wintergreen, on a cool forest floor. Or when one's cry of joy was transposed into gull clamour by a sea wind pungent with the scent of rotting kelp. When one sought, and found; when one relinquished, and was free.

The quality of wildness remains in us. It is masked from our awareness in multifarious ways, including our own conscious rejection. We are "different," but not perhaps in ways the humanists would prefer. We are different from Nature in that we are domesticated and culturally conditioned, and that we depend upon a fabricated prosthesis to function in an ideology-dependent universe we have ourselves created. But ideologies change.

Look at a child gently holding an unfledged young robin that has fallen from its nest. Look in that child's eyes. The sweet bondage of wildness is recoverable.

ΠOTES

PREFACE

1. The pulse of this activity is thoughtfully monitored in *The Trumpeter*, a quarterly journal edited by Alan R. Drengson, P.O. Box 5853, Station B, Victoria, British Columbia V8R 6S8.
2. D.E. Davis, in *ECOphilosophy: A Field Guide to the Literature*, provides an extremely useful and comprehensive bibliography. Entries are of necessity brief, but the most significant "landmarks" are well displayed. Davis intends to produce updated revisions. Warwick Fox, in *Toward a Transpersonal Ecology*, furnishes a thorough and indispensable account and analysis of "deep ecology" thinking to date.
3. Much Aquarian, New Age, and Gaian material, for example, smacks of old anthropocentrist wine in new "environmentalist" bottles.
4. Paul Shepard, in *Nature and Madness*, characterizes Western civilization as one of arrested development, and of madness. Neil Evernden, in *The Natural Alien: Humankind and Environment*, describes us as "natural aliens." Shepard's vehicle is psychohistory; Evernden's, phenomenology. I am influenced by both.

THE PROBLEM ANIMAL

1. Dale A. Russell, in *An Odyssey in Time: the Dinosaurs of North America*, reviews the evidence.
2. Being a "top" predator is rather like being a first-class baseball player. A batting average of .350 means that the hitter is unsuccessful 65% of the time. The analogy is reasonable. I once estimated a female cheetah supporting small young at .333.

3. On wants and needs, see especially Herbert Marcuse, *One-Dimensional Man*, and William Leiss, *The Limits to Satisfaction*. On advertising and manipulation, see William Leiss, Stephen Kline, and Sut Jhally, *Social Communication in Advertising*.

4. Charles F. Hockett and Robert Ascher, "The Human Revolution."

5. In my *Arctic Oil*, pp. 109–11, I apply Romer's Rule to energy supplies in the contemporary industrial growth society.

6. My "Ethics as Prosthetics." Even such a modest metaphoric venture can generate heat in many quarters. See, for example, J. Andrew Brook, "Ethics and Survival."

7. Robert K. Merton, in his foreword to Jacques Ellul's *The Technological Society*, p. vi. I am using "technology" as meaning the study and knowledge of technique so defined.

8. In our technoculture, if a problem cannot be defined in terms of a technical solution, it usually cannot be defined at all. Even more depressing is the observation that our fixation on solutions is indicative of our enmeshment in mechanistic thinking. As John Wilkinson, translator of Ellul's *The Technological Society*, says, "It is... *the essence of technique to compel the qualitative to become the quantitative*" (p. xvi, emphasis his).

PROSTHETIC BEING

1. The popular interpretations, and the general consternation, were inspired by the exceedingly readable and provocative work of Robert Ardrey (*African Genesis* and *The Territorial Imperative*), and Konrad Lorenz (*On Aggression*). Antidotes, for those who required them, were soon provided by Ashley Montagu (*Man and Aggression*), Anthony Storr (*Human Aggression* and *Human Destructiveness*), and Hans Kummer (*Primate Societies*), among numerous others.

2. Paul Shepard, in *The Tender Carnivore and the Sacred Game*, calls the dawn of agriculture "the invention of drudgery and catastrophe" (p. 16). Jared Diamond, in "The Worst Mistake in the History of the Human Race," provides his opinion of it in the title of his article.

3. Peter Wilson, in *The Domestication of the Human Species*, sees human domestication as "the adoption of the built environment" (p. 9) — sedentism with the fabrication of dwellings. As I do, he feels

that this antedated the domestication of plants and animals; his perspective, however, is that of an anthropologist; mine is that of a naturalist.

4. T. Tennessen and R.J. Hudson, "Traits Relevant to the Domestication of Herbivores." A selective feeder, such as a deer, is very particular about the twigs and shoots it browses. Cattle and goats, by contrast, will graze over a wide spectrum of plants. We humans and our antecedents appear to have been non-selective omnivores for a very long time.

5. L. David Mech, *The Wolf*, p. 111.

6. Barry Lopez, in *Of Wolves and Men*, calls this "ceremonial exchange" the "conversation of death," in which animals "appear to lock eyes and make a decision" (p. 94).

7. Konrad Lorenz, *King Soloman's Ring*, p. 135.

8. Helmut Hemmer, in *Domestication: The Decline of Environmental Appreciation*, postulates northern and southern forms of the wolf, with the dog ancestor as the latter, a more "primitive" population.

9. It is said, however, that the pig may well be the equal of the dog in both of these respects. I have no evidence to offer.

10. Hemmer, in *Domestication*, speaks of the perceptual impoverishment of the domesticated animal as the loss of "environmental appreciation," a shrinkage of its *Merkwelt*.

11. Richard E. Leakey and Roger Lewin, *Origins*, p. 197.

12. Leakey and Lewin, ibid., p. 131, describe "heat-charred stones and earth on a campsite east of Lake Turkana that goes back some two and a half million years" and go on to say that "whether these are the remains of a deliberately made fire while the camp was occupied, or are merely the result of an accidental fire which burned on the site after it had been abandoned, we cannot be sure."

13. John A. Livingston, *One Cosmic Instant: A Natural History of Human Arrogance*, p. 132.

14. Ibid.

15. Carl O. Sauer, in "The Agency of Man on the Earth," says: "When humans lost the oestrus cycle is unknown; its weakening and loss is probably a feature of domestication, and it may have occurred early in the history of man, eldest of the domesticated creatures" (p. 50).

16. Arthur Koestler, *The Ghost in the Machine*, pp. 260–61.

THE EXOTIC TRANSPLANTS

1. We have long since had to abandon such items as tool use, tool making, language, abstraction, and culture.
2. I use the term "separation"; others of a different bent might see it as expulsion; many certainly see it as emancipation.
3. Charles S. Elton, *The Ecology of Invasions by Animals and Plants*.
4. Ibid., p. 31.
5. W. Earl Godfrey, *The Birds of Canada*, p. 574.
6. Other areas of the world have not been so fortunate with introductions. In Hawaii, for example, thirty species of exotic small birds have had the effect of eliminating twenty-five native species.
7. Allen Keast, *Australia and the Pacific Islands*, p. 86.
8. Clive Roots, *Animal Invaders*, p. 76.
9. Ibid., p. 75.
10. Wapiti (North America), red deer (Europe), sike (Japan), fallow deer (Asia Minor), ruse deer (Indonesia), sambar (India), white-tailed deer (North America).
11. In the sensitive high alpine grasslands of the central-southern Alps of New Zealand, thar were hunted commercially until 1983. During the ensuing six years, their numbers dwindled.
12. Roots, *Animal Invaders*.
13. Ibid., p. 94.
14. Ibid., p. 96.
15. A. de Vos, R.H. Manville, and R.G. Van Gelder, "Introduced Mammals and Their Influence on Native Biota"; Elton, *The Ecology of Invasions by Animals and Plants*; George Laycock, *The Alien Animals*; and Roots, *Animal Invaders*, detail the horror stories.
16. Most nature preservationists condemn the goat out of hand. For an interesting, but heavily management-oriented minority opinion, see Robin Dunbar, "Scapegoat for a Thousand Deserts." Dunbar argues that "the blame for most of the evils heaped onto the goat's shoulders lie [sic] in the poor management and husbandry practices of their owners."
17. Various islands also harbour free-running cattle and pigs, horses, donkeys, cats, and dogs. The damage done by each of these is different from place to place, but all have wreaked havoc.
18. Eugene Odum, in *Basic Ecology*, suggests that this "combination of

artificial and natural selection seems to produce plants and animals that thrive in habitats that have been partially altered or disturbed" (p. 482). The feral domesticate would appear to derive the best from both worlds, natural communities to inherit the worst.

19. Nomad Films International, in *The Intruders*, reports feral goats shot in the Flinders ranges of southern Australia that "weighed up to 160 pounds with a horn spread of more than 3 feet" from a population of more than 30,000 in that area.

20. From an editorial in *International Journal for Studies in Animal Problems* 4/3 (1983).

21. Paul Ehrlich and Ann Ehrlich, *Extinction*, p. 133.

22. The literature focusing on this debate is considerable. Paul S. Martin and H.E. Wright, Jr., eds., *Pleistocene Extinctions: The Search for a Cause*, is the primary source. Leigh Van Valen, "Late Pleistocene Extinctions" reviews the debate itself. See also Prince Philip, Duke of Edinburgh, and James Fisher, *Wildlife Crisis*, pp. 116–208, in which Fisher presents the evidence continent by continent; John A. Livingston, *One Cosmic Instant: A Natural History of Human Arrogance*, pp. 122–32; and Erhlich and Erhlich, *Extinction*, pp. 130–34.

23. Prince Philip and Fisher, *Wildlife Crisis*, p. 165.

24. Norman Myers, *The Sinking Ark*, p. 4.

25. Ibid., p. 5.

THE EXOTIC IDEOLOGY

1. An ecotype is a locally adapted population of a widespread species, a potential race.

2. Perhaps this the place to note that there is no such animal as a "primitive" human being or human society. We are all of the same evolutionary age, all of the same lineage, all of the same stuff. The use of "primitive" in respect to human beings and societies, or indeed any other aspect of Nature, bespeaks the colossal deterministic arrogance of Euro-American ideology.

3. They have also been devastating for humankind, according to Paul Shepard (*The Tender Carnivore and the Sacred Game* and *Nature and Madness*), in both environmental and psychosocial terms. These unique works are essential reading in matters of subsistence hunting,

agriculture, and the legacy of the latter for "civilization."

4. The name is slightly misleading. Although we see these birds hanging around cattle, they naturally accompany buffalo, rhinos, elephants, and the larger antelopes. Even in Asia and Africa today, they have little but cattle to which to attach themselves. It has been suggested that the wide dispersal of this heron may have been facilitated by the spread of domesticated herds. I think it is more likely a manifestation of the vast distribution of very many species of big ungulates in prehuman times. In the Americas, it found nothing *but* cattle.

5. Joseph Meeker, *The Comedy of Survival*, pp. 70–72. The term was coined by Erik H. Erikson.

6. Ibid., p. 71.

7. The word "environmental" is used here in its broad sense, to include both sociocultural and ecological contexts. As with other exotic introductions, no one seems to know why one transplant will "take" and another fail, in the same or different places, at the same or different times.

8. Juliet Clutton-Brock, in *Domesticated Animals from Early Times*, provides a comprehensive account of all species from the archaeological evidence.

9. In the early 1990s, the international mercantile buzzword had become "globalization."

10. Certainly the Christian missionaries were casting their nets to capture souls for salvation, but in doing so they were admirably serving the expansionist interests of their imperial sponsors.

11. Some insight into the technoculture's commodification of all living things is conveyed in the term "human resources."

12. The image of "rape" is often used to describe the industrial pillaging of Nature. This is quite inappropriate. Rape is the violation of a person's right to consent or not to consent to an act. Nature has no right to such a choice.

13. Wolfgang Sachs, "The Archaeology of the Development Idea."

14. The foregoing discussion of "development" appears in modified form in my "Nature for the Sake of Nature," p. 241.

15. Sachs, "The Archaeology of the Development Idea."

16. David Ehrenfeld, *The Arrogance of Humanism*, p. 59. Examples and elaboration run throughout this intensely valuable work.

17. Karl Popper, *The Poverty of Historicism*, p. 3 (emphasis his).
18. Bryan Magee, *Popper*, pp. 98–99.
19. Donald Worster, *Nature's Economy: The Roots of Ecology*, p. 299.
20. Eugene Odum, *Basic Ecology*, p. 372.
21. Eugene Odum, *Ecology and Our Endangered Life-Support Systems*, p. 165.
22. Odum, *Basic Ecology*, p. 373.
23. The terms "resource" and "exploitation" are universally used in ecology.
24. Paul Colinvaux, *Ecology*, p. 712.
25. Worster, *Nature's Economy*, p. 299.
26. See ibid., pp. 298–99, for an excellent discussion of the origin and evolution of the concept of "niche."
27. As Neil Evernden is wont to remark, the human species fancies itself not only as omniscient but also as "omnichient."
28. In an interview on development for the Canadian Broadcasting Corporation's radio series *Ideas*, written and produced by David Cayley, 1990.

Nature's Marketplace

1. Oversimply put, Darwinian natural selection is about the environmental constraints or opportunities that cause extinctions and allow the emergence of new species. If a species "fits" its environment it will survive. If it does not, it will disappear. Those that survive have been selected in; those that do not have been selected out. Environments change, and selective screens change accordingly, allowing the emergence of new forms. Darwin saw selective forces within and between species as competition. He knew nothing of genetics. Today, science accepts the fact of speciation by natural selection; most modern studies are concerned with how it works.
2. There are many detailed accounts of Darwin's indebtedness to the social thought of his time, and of the process and structure of his synthesis. Among these, especially valuable are Donald Worster's *Nature's Economy: The Roots of Ecology*, and John Greene's *Science, Ideology, and World View*.
3. Greene, *Science, Ideology, and World View*, p. 124.
4. Ibid., p. 7.

5. Charles Darwin, *On the Origin of Species*, p. 62. The 1964 Harvard University Press edition is a facsimile of the 1859 first edition of *Origin*, with an introduction by Ernst Mayr.
6. Ibid., p. 110.
7. Ibid., p. 111.
8. Ibid., p. 337.
9. Ibid., p. 472.
10. Greene, *Science, Ideology, and World View*, p. 150.
11. Darwin, *On the Origin of Species*, p. 490.
12. Konrad Lorenz, *On Aggression*, p. 45.
13. Thorlief Schjelderup-Ebbe, "Beitrage zur Sozialpsychologie des Haushuhns."
14. It is my developed suspicion that *all* aggression is defensive. When it is offensive, it is pathological.
15. As well, ironically enough, robust in the literature of economics are "predation" and "parasitism," which in biology are neutral, but in human affairs are loaded terms.
16. But this is not to say that self-awareness need in any sense necessitate a competitive orientation.
17. This example, from the area in which I live, also draws upon some series described by Eugene Odum in *Basic Ecology*, pp. 456–62.
18. Such interpretations dominate the contemporary ecological literature. These examples are from Paul Colinvaux, in *Ecology*, pp. 588–89. Although ecologists freely acknowledge that they are using loaded terms, and all the best texts offer such acknowledgment (invoking the interest of ready communication), the underlying "thrust" of the competitive economic bias is relentless.
19. Darwin, *On the Origin of Species*, p. 62; Worster *Nature's Economy*, p. 144.
20. A little later, Leakey's female students became "trimates" with the addition of orangutan researcher and defender Biruté Galdikas.
21. Goodall's popular book *In the Shadow of Man* reveals in the title the normal human (male?) chauvinist position. Fossey's *Gorillas in the Mist* says more about the author. The scientific publications of both are straight-line and largely non-controversial.
22. Leakey was a superenergetic, rollicking enthusiast. I have fond memories of convivial occasions in London, Toronto, and Nairobi,

but especially at Olduvai Gorge, where he showed me my first purple grenadier — one of the brilliant little African finches.

23. Thelma Rowell, "The Concept of Dominance."

24. Gorillas are very peaceful, usually quiet, animals. Fights do occur, but they are exceptional. Male "rank" is based on age, according to Kelly J. Stewart and Alexander H. Harcourt, in Smuts, Barbara, et al., p. 159 "Gorillas: Variation in Female Relationships." One of Fossey's silverback friends was severely wounded by a male from a neighbouring group: Farley Mowat, *Virunga: The Passion of Dian Fossey*, p. 364.

25. Smuts, Barbara, et al. *Primate Societies*, p. 159.

26. Ibid., p. 346.

27. Stewart and Harcourt, "Gorillas," pp. 158–59.

28. A number of years ago, a British television crew filmed male olive baboons in "combat." Individuals frequently chase one another, and make a fearsome racket while doing so. Often there is a wild and terrifying mêlée when they make contact. The TV film showed one of these whirling, tumbling "fights" just as it happened, complete with blood-curdling screeches and roars, then showed it again in slow motion. What was *actually* happening was a gymnastic tumbling performance outshining any Chinese circus act. So far as one could see, the two individuals never in fact touched each other! But their gyrations and flips and turns were so blindingly fast, and their voices so terrifying, that had the film not been slowed down, the aggressively competitive stereotype would have remained firmly in place.

29. This happened in Sri Lanka, the original isle of Serendib. As with the Kenyan baboons, I was in the company of Nancy Archibald and Rudi Kovanic of the Canadian Broadcasting Corporation's *The Nature of Things*.

30. It is interesting that infanticide by the male grey langurs has been interpreted by a female primatologist as male genetic politics (insuring that his own genes replace those of his most recent predecessor), and by a male primatologist as a response to crowding and food shortage. Such interpretations are, of course, objective and value-free.

31. Rowell, "The Concept of Dominance."

32. With special emphasis on gender "roles" in primate social organization, Altmann, Fedigan, Haraway, Herschberger, Hrdy, Rowell, Smuts, Strum, and Zihlman are among the pre-eminent names. There are many more. These women have been and are in the process not only of turning the Euro-American male "paradigm" inside out, but of leaving it in shreds. Their approach to critical analysis is very like that employed by "deep ecology."

33. Linda Marie Fedigan, *Primate Paradigms: Sex Roles and Social Bonds*, p. 94.

34. Stephen Clark, *The Nature of the Beast: Are Animals Moral?*, p. 112.

35. For a pleasant summary of the historic literature and later interpretations, see Joel Carl Welty., *The Life of Birds*, pp. 209–27.

36. It should be remembered that, in our inherited tradition, the most fundamental of rights is the right to own property. More anthropomorphic projection.

37. Neil Evernden, *The Natural Alien: Humankind and Environment*, p. 44.

38. Ibid., pp. 73–102.

39. Fights do happen, not only between cardinals but also between gorillas and between baboons and between people. But in non-humans they are very uncommon. Nobody is perfect.

40. I am grateful to Neil Evernden (personal communication) for this distinction.

41. Mowat, *Virunga*.

OTHER SELVES

1. John Livingston, "Nature for the Sake of Nature," p. 245.

2. R.A. Gardner and B.T. Gardner, "Teaching Sign Language to a Chimpanzee." Washoe was followed by a series of chimps, gorillas, and orangutans who learned signing and some of whom taught it to their and others' children. Perhaps the most famous of these were the orang Princess, who taught signing to a human child, and the gorilla Koko, who invented jokes and insults, prompted answers in tests for her younger companion gorilla, reported past events in her life, had a vulgar sense of humour, kept pets, photographed herself with a Polaroid camera in a mirror, identified herself in the picture, and signed "Love camera": Donna Haraway, *Primate Visions:*

Gender, Race and Nature in the World of Modern Science, pp. 141–43.

3. Neil Evernden (personal communication) reminds me that this is what he would call the "ego."
4. It has been suggested to me that similar questions might be asked about the mass behaviour of crowds at football games or rock concerts, in which unison so often prevails. My answer is that the domesticates in the bleachers have been well and truly conditioned to respond to certain cues — good or bad plays on the field, punctuations in the rock performance. They *expect* those cues, and are prepared for them. This is what I like to call domesticated "followership." Watch the trained reflexes at any political convention.
5. Paul Shepard and Barry Sanders, *The Sacred Paw: The Bear in Nature, Myth, and Literature*, p. 8.
6. Neil Evernden, *The Natural Alien: Humankind and Environment*, pp. 35–54.
7. For an exhaustive and brilliantly argued analysis of this, with emphasis on primatology, see Haraway, *Primate Visions*.
8. The notion of "participating consciousness" originates with Owen Barfield, in *Saving the Appearances*, and is developed in Morris Berman's *The Reenchantment of the World*.
9. The process as described here would apply to most mammals and many birds, but not all. There will be great differences between species and groups of species. These will manifest themselves chiefly in the relative (not absolute) length of infancy and childhood, and in the degree of group sociality characteristic of the species.
10. Population, in ecology, a term "originally coined to denote a group of people, is broadened to include groups of individuals of any one kind of organism": Eugene Odum, *Basic Ecology*, p. 4.
11. Gregory Bateson, *Steps to an Ecology of Mind*, pp. 38–39.
12. In high latitudes, the changing duration of daylight is obviously important; in low latitudes, it is much less so.

KIDS' STUFF

1. Paul Shepard, *Nature and Madness*, p. 109.
2. Shephard (personal communication), a revision of the diagram in

Shepard, *Nature and Madness*, p. 111.

3. Ibid.

4. Shepard, *Nature and Madness*, p. 109.

5. Joel Carl Welty, *The Life of Birds*, p. 178.

6. Ibid., p. 178.

7. Sara J. Shettleworth, "Learning and Behavioural Ecology," citing P.P.G. Bateson, "How Do Sensitive Periods Arise and What Are They For?"

8. Perhaps at this stage, oral tactility is more informative than that derived from other sense organs. There is often very much mouthing without apparent damage to the captive.

9. "Classification is a condition for cognition; cognition in turn dispels classification": Max Horkheimer and Theodor Adorno, *Dialectic of Enlightenment*, p. 220.

10. Edith Cobb, "The Ecology of Imagination in Childhood."

11. Ibid.

12. Ibid.

13. Antoine de Saint Exupéry, *The Little Prince*, p. 53.

14. R.D. Laing, *The Politics of Experience*, pp. 22–23.

15. George Grant, *Technology and Justice*, p. 32.

16. John A. Livingston, *The Fallacy of Wildlife Conservation*, pp. 92–97.

17. Laing, *The Politics of Experience*, p. 61.

ZERO-ORDER HUMANISM

1. As I suggested in *The Fallacy of Wildlife Conservation*, p. 103, humankind stands to Nature as intellect to emotion, reason to experience.

2. David Ehrenfeld, *The Arrogance of Humanism*, pp. 5–6.

3. Northrop Frye, *The Great Code*, p. 37.

4. Ibid., p. 49.

5. No political ideology, of whatever hue, is exempt from the dominance of zero-order humanism. This point is developed in "Sweet Bondage."

6. See William Leiss's *The Domination of Nature* for a benchmark account of the *idea* of the mastery of Nature from Francis Bacon to the contemporary role of science and technology.

7. Pierre Teilhard de Chardin's *The Phenomenon of Man* and *Man's Place in Nature*, for example, in which human consciousness (knowing) will "infallibly" constitute the culmination of evolution and the ultimate destiny of Earth.

8. There is much of this material about. For an entirely satisfactory and representative example, see Norman Myers, ed., *GAIA: An Atlas of Planet Management*, the final section of which is titled "Under New Management." J.E. Lovelock, in *Gaia, a New Look at Life on Earth*, provides the neo-Teilhardian rationale, suggesting that only through human agency does planet Earth become whole and complete, self-aware in the human image. Popularizations such as Toffler's *The Third Wave* have enjoyed tremendous commercial success. There is an immense market for zero-order humanism.

9. International Union for the Conservation of Nature, *The World Conservation Strategy*.

10. The World Commission on Environment and Development, *Our Common Future*, a direct lineal descendent of Barbara Ward and Rene Dubos's *Only One Earth*, which was prepared for the United Nations Conference on the Human Environment.

11. I am indebted to my son John R. Livingston for this metaphor. See his "The World Conservation Strategy as a Dystopian Vision," an analysis of the World Conservation Strategy as a dystopian vision in terms of George Orwell and Aldous Huxley.

12. John Dewey, *Experience and Nature*, p. 382.

13. There was once a *lottery* on behalf of "mental health." I shall not pursue that here.

14. There are many sources. See especially Peter Singer, *Animal Liberation*; Stanley Godlovitch, Rosalind Godlovitch, and John Harris, eds., *Animals, Men and Morals*; and in less literally vivid but even more revealing terms, Bernard Rollin, *The Unheeded Cry*.

15. Both are systematically, exhaustively, and readably addressed by Rollin in *Animal Rights and Human Morality* and especially *The Unheeded Cry*.

16. The Canadian Department of External Affairs retained a public relations firm from Washington, D.C., to advise on the best ways to promote the interests of the industry and reduce the influence of the anti-fur lobby.

211

17. This and other research sponsored by the Federal-Provincial Committee for Humane Trapping is summarized by Milan Novak et al., in *Wild Furbearer Management and Conservation in North America*, pp. 964–65.

18. *Skinned*, edited by Anne Doncaster, is a collection of authoritative essays in condemnation of commerce in fur from a variety of points of view, with emphasis on the "deconstruction" of the received mythology.

19. Thanks to the unflagging efforts of animal welfare organizations, there has been some recent progress in the use of *in vitro* experimental techniques in pharmaceutical, cosmetic, and even medical research. There remains, however, a very long way to go.

20. The word "pet" connotes a possession or commodity, an adjunct to the human self-image. Those of us who love our family dogs as unique and distinct individuals usually prefer the term "companion animal."

21. None of this is to suggest that zoos do not or cannot at least occasionally inspire young people to see animals as *subjects* worthy of their serious — sometimes lifelong — attention. This happens.

22. Until I learned better from a good dog instructor, I would push a puppy's rump down to the floor and portentously intone "*SIT.*" Now I wait until the puppy sits of its own accord, and brightly and conversationally remark "Sit." It takes half the time for the dog to learn, costs nothing in frustration for either of us, and allows the dog to do precisely what it wants to do — participate and cooperate. Judiciously administered treats help.

23. In Calgary in 1986, nine horses were killed in a single such race.

24. According to *The Globe and Mail* of Saturday, July 14, 1990, more than a million people attend the Calgary Exhibition and Stampede each year, "injecting between $80-million and $90-million into the local economy. The Stampede has also become a symbol that gives Calgary an international reputation as a place where the Wild West is still alive and well."

25. Elizabeth Atwood Lawrence, *Rodeo*, p. 270.

26. James Serpell, *In the Company of Animals: A Study of Human–Animal Relationships*, p. 179.

NATURAL RIGHTS

1. Uwe Porksen, on the Canadian Broadcasting Corporation's *Ideas* series, calls them "plastic words": words which once had precise meaning in precise contexts, and which still carry the ring of authority even though they have been largely emptied of meaning through indiscriminate popular usage. He singles out words such as "development," "sexuality," "information," "growth," "value," etc. To his list we would add "environment," "ecology," "nature," and the like.
2. The historical effect of the fashion fur trade on indigenous societies and cultures cannot be overstated.
3. Cynthia Giagnocavo, "Legal Strategies and the Reconstruction of an Environmental Ethic."
4. The many formulas and recipes which have been advanced cannot be listed here. Among the more bizarre have been efforts to create "Linnean" taxonomies which would indicate which forms (vertebrates only? mammals only? large mammals only? etc.) would qualify. A sort of hierarchical Great Chain of Being with a cut-off line between the haves and the have nots, the deserving and the undeserving.
5. Peter Singer, *Animal Liberation*.
6. Ibid., pp. 254–55.
7. Ibid., p. 255.
8. Ibid.
9. Ibid., p. 256.
10. Bernard Rollin, *Animal Rights and Human Morality*, pp. 72–73.
11. Ibid., p. 39.
12. Ibid., p. 74.
13. Ibid., p. 81.
14. Ibid., p. 86.
15. Rollin, *Animal Rights and Human Morality* and *The Unheeded Cry*.
16. Christopher Stone, "Should Trees Have Standing? — Toward Legal Rights for Natural Objects."
17. Ibid.
18. Richard Routley and Val Routley, "Human Chauvinism and Environmental Ethics," p. 109.

19. John A. Livingston, "Rightness or Rights?," as part of a legal journal symposium on law and ecological ethics.
20. Ibid., p. 320.
21. Thomas Birch, "The Incarceration of Wildness: Wilderness Areas as Prisons."
22. Livingston, "Rightness or Rights?," p. 321.
23. Giagnocavo, in "Legal Strategies and the Reconstruction of an Environmental Ethic," p. 51, reminds us that "[Martin Luther] King was not speaking of rights but rather of *rightness*. King's distinction was between 'just and unjust' laws; in other words he suggested that rights are ultimately a question of rightness."

SWEET BONDAGE

1. Even when run feral, they depend upon our having prepared the way for them by our own prior ecological simplification.
2. There is a very considerable literature on this subject, most but not all of it addressing intrahuman affairs. Two outstanding contributions from the psychoanalytic point of view are Anthony Storr's *Human Destructiveness* and Erich Fromm's *The Anatomy of Human Destructiveness*. Paul Shepard, in a unique and original analysis (*Nature and Madness*), uses child development and psychohistory. "Innate human aggressiveness" has been pretty well shelved since the 1960s, and not a moment too soon.
3. The overwhelming thrust of the "environmental" movement is dedicated not to the interest of Nature, but to the security and sustainability of the advancement of the human enterprise.
4. Shepard, *Nature and Madness*, p. 129.
5. Ibid., p. 130.
6. Ibid., p. 129.
7. Fromm, in *The Anatomy of Human Destructiveness*, pp. 129–81, provides an interesting summary of the anthropological evidence, centred on aggression.
8. Alfie Kohn, *No Contest: The Case Against Competition*, although mostly devoted to contemporary American society, sheds invaluable light on cultural conditioning.
9. This brief discussion of the future appeared originally in different form in my "Les implications écologiques du caractère impératif de

l'immortalité d l'homme."

10. Shepard, *Nature and Madness.*
11. Arne Naess, "The Shallow and the Deep, Long-Range Ecology Movement."
12. Bill Devall, "Reformist Environmentalism."
13. The nature of environmentalism is revealed through brilliant dissection in Neil Evernden's *The Natural Alien: Humankind and Environment.*
14. Robyn Eckersley, "The Road to Ecotopia? Socialism versus Environmentalism."
15. Ibid.
16. George Sessions, "Ecocentrism and the Greens: Deep Ecology and the Environmental Task."
17. An important new contribution is Paul Ehrlich and Ann Ehrlich, *The Population Explosion.*
18. As a few samples only, but indicative of the trend, see William Vogt, *Road to Survival*; Robert Cook, *Human Fertility: The Modern Dilemma*; Marston Bates, *The Prevalence of People*; Georg Borgstrom, *The Hungry Planet: The Modern World at the Edge of Famine* and *Too Many*; Paul Ehrlich, *The Population Bomb*; and Henry Regier and J. Bruce Falls, eds., *Exploding Humanity.*
19. Vogt, *Road to Survival*, pp. x–xi.
20. A term originating with military field medicine. When facilities are limited, wounded are divided into three groups: (a) those who will not survive whether they receive care or not; (b) those who will survive whether they receive immediate care or not; (c) those who will survive if given immediate care. The priority goes to group (c), maximizing the number of lives saved.
21. Robert Heilbroner, *An Inquiry into the Human Prospect*, p. 35.
22. Ibid.
23. J. Stan Rowe, *Home Place: Essays on Ecology*, p. 125.
24. The line, "That sweet bondage which is freedom's self" from *Queen Mab*, comes from one who did not know about the ties of interdependence that sustain free and wild natural societies. He did, however, know about the privileges and obligations of the eighteenth-century democratic ideal. And he knew about love.

SELECTED

BIBLIOGRAPHY

Ardrey, Robert. *African Genesis*. New York: Atheneum, 1961.

_____. *The Territorial Imperative*. New York: Dell Publishing, 1966.

Barfield, Owen. *Saving the Appearances*. New York: Harcourt, Brace and World, 1965.

Bates, Marston. *The Prevalence of People*. New York: Charles Scribner's Sons, 1962.

Bateson, Gregory. *Steps to an Ecology of Mind*. New York: Ballantine Books, 1972.

Bateson, P.P.G. "How Do Sensitive Periods Arise and What Are They For?" *Animal Behaviour* 27 (1979): 480–86.

Berger, John. *Ways of Seeing*. Harmondsworth: Penguin, 1972.

Bergman, Charles. *Wild Echoes: Encounters with the Most Endangered Animals in North America*. New York: McGraw-Hill, 1990.

Berman, Morris. *The Reenchantment of the World*. Ithaca, N.Y.: Cornell University Press, 1981.

Birch, Charles, and John B. Cobb, Jr. *The Liberation of Life*. Cambridge: Cambridge University Press, 1981.

Birch, Thomas H. "The Incarceration of Wildness: Wilderness Areas as Prisons." *Environmental Ethics* 12 (Spring 1990).

Borgstrom, Georg. *The Hungry Planet: The Modern World at the Edge of Famine*. New York: Macmillan, 1965.

_____. *Too Many*. New York: Collier Books, 1971.

Brook, J. Andrew. "Ethics and Survival," In Philip P. Hanson, ed., *Environmental Ethics: Philosophical and Policy Perspectives*. Burnaby, B.C.: Simon Fraser University, 1986.

Brownlee, A. *Biological Complimentariness: A Study of Evolution*. Edinburgh: A. Brownlee, 1981.

Clark, Stephen R.L. *The Nature of the Beast: Are Animals Moral?* Oxford: Oxford University Press, 1982.

Clutton-Brock, Juliet. *Domesticated Animals from Early Times*. London: Heinemann and British Museum (Natural History), 1981.

Cobb, Edith. "The Ecology of Imagination in Childhood." *Daedalus* 88/3 (Summer 1959), 537–48.

Colinvaux, Paul. *Ecology*. New York: John Wiley and Sons, 1986.

Cook, Robert C. *Human Fertility: The Modern Dilemma*. London: Victor Gollancz, 1951.

Crosby, Alfred W. *Ecological Imperialism: The Biological Expansion of Europe, 900-1900*. Cambridge: Cambridge University Press, 1986.

Darwin, Charles. *On the Origin of Species*. Cambridge, Mass.: Harvard University Press, 1964.

Davis, Donald Edward. *ECOphilosophy: A Field Guide to the Literature*. San Pedro, Cal.: R. and E. Miles, 1989.

Devall, Bill. "Reformist Environmentalism." *Humboldt Journal of Social Relations* 6/2 (Spring 1979).

_____. "Deep Ecology and its Critics." The Trumpeter 5/2 (Spring 1988).

de Vos, A., R.H. Manville, and R.G. Van Gelder. "Introduced Mammals and Their Influence on Native Biota." *Zoologica* 41 (1956), 163–94.

Dewey, John. *Experience and Nature*. New York: Dover Publications, 1958.

Diamond, Jared. "The Worst Mistake in the History of the Human Race." *Discover*, May 1987.

Doncaster, Anne, ed. *Skinned*. North Falmouth, Mass. and Mississauga, Ont.: International Wildlife Coalition, 1988.

Dunbar, Robin. "Scapegoat for a Thousand Deserts." *New Scientist* 15, November 1984.

Eckersley, Robyn. "The Road to Ecotopia? Socialism versus Environmentalism." *The Trumpeter* 5/2 (Spring 1988).

Ehrenfeld, David. *The Arrogance of Humanism*. New York: Oxford University Press, 1978.

Ehrlich, Paul. *The Population Bomb.* New York: Ballantine Books, 1968.

Ehrlich, Paul, and Ann Ehrlich. *Extinction.* New York: Ballantine Books, 1981.

_____. *The Population Explosion.* New York: Simon and Schuster, 1990.

Ellul, Jacques. *The Technological Society.* New York: Random House, 1964.

Elton, Charles S. *The Ecology of Invasions by Animals and Plants.* London: Methuen, 1958.

Evernden, Neil, ed. *The Paradox of Environmentalism.* Toronto: Faculty of Environmental Studies, York University, 1984.

_____. *The Natural Alien: Humankind and Environment.* Toronto: University of Toronto Press, 1985.

_____. *The Social Creation of Nature.* Baltimore: Johns Hopkins University Press, 1992.

Fedigan, Linda Marie. *Primate Paradigms: Sex Roles and Social Bonds.* Montreal: Eden Press, 1982.

Fossey, Dian. *Gorillas in the Mist.* Boston: Houghton Mifflin, 1983.

Fox, Warwick. *Toward a Transpersonal Ecology.* Boston: Shambhala, 1990.

Fromm, Erich. *The Anatomy of Human Destructiveness.* New York: Holt, Rinehart and Winston, 1973.

Frye, Northrop. *The Great Code.* New York: Harcourt Brace Jovanovich, 1982.

Gardner, R.A., and B.T. Gardner. "Teaching Sign Language to a Chimpanzee." *Science* 165 (1969), 664–72.

Giagnocavo, Cynthia L. "Legal Strategies and the Reconstruction of an Environmental Ethic." Unpublished M.E.S. thesis, Faculty of Environmental Studies, York University, 1992.

Godfrey, W. Earl. *The Birds of Canada.* Ottawa: National Museums of Canada, 1986.

Godlovitch, Stanley, Roslind Godlovitch, and John Harris, eds. *Animals, Men and Morals.* London: Victor Gollancz, 1971.

Goodall, Jane [van Lawick]. *In the Shadow of Man.* Boston: Houghton Mifflin, 1971.

Grant, George. *Technology and Justice.* Toronto: Anansi, 1986.

Greene, John C. *Science, Ideology, and World View.* Berkeley, Cal.: University of California Press, 1981.

Haraway, Donna. *Primate Visions: Gender, Race and Nature in the World of Modern Science*. New York: Routledge, 1989.

Hearne, Vicki. Adam's Task: *Calling Animals by Name*. New York: Alfred A. Knopf, 1987.

Heilbroner, Robert L. *An Inquiry into the Human Prospect*. New York: W.W. Norton and Company, 1974.

Hemmer, Helmut. *Domestication: The Decline of Environmental Appreciation*. Cambridge: Cambridge University Press, 1990.

Hockett, Charles F., and Robert Ascher. "The Human Revolution." *Current Anthropology 5* (1964), 135–68.

Horkheimer, Max, and Theodor Adorno. *Dialectic of Enlightenment*. New York: Continuum, 1987.

International Union for the Conservation of Nature. *The World Conservation Strategy*. 1980.

Keast, Allen. *Australia and the Pacific Islands*. New York: Random House, 1966.

Koestler, Arthur. *The Ghost in the Machine*. London: Pan Books, 1975.

Kohn, Alfie. *No Contest: The Case Against Competition*. Boston: Houghton Mifflin, 1986.

Kummer, Hans. *Primate Societies*. Chicago: Aldine Atherton, 1971.

Laing, R.D. *The Politics of Experience*. Harmondsworth: Penguin, 1967.

Laycock, George. *The Alien Animals*. Garden City, N.Y.: Natural History Press, 1966.

Lawrence, Elizabeth Atwood. *Rodeo*. Knoxville: The University of Tennessee Press, 1982.

Leakey, Richard E., and Roger Lewin. *Origins*. New York: E.P. Dutton, 1977.

Leiss, William. *The Domination of Nature*. New York: George Braziller, 1972.

_____. *The Limits to Satisfaction*. Toronto: University of Toronto Press, 1976.

Leiss, William, Stephen Kline, and Sut Jhally. *Social Communication in Advertising*. Toronto: Methuen, 1986.

Livingston, John A. *One Cosmic Instant: A Natural History of Human Arrogance*. Toronto: McClelland and Stewart, 1973.

_____. *Arctic Oil*. Toronto: Canadian Broadcasting Corporation, 1981.

_____. *The Fallacy of Wildlife Conservation*. Toronto: McClelland and

Stewart, 1981.

_____. "Rightness or Rights?" *Osgoode Hall Law Journal* 22/2 (Summer 1984).

_____. "Ethics as Prosthetics." In Philip P. Hanson, ed., *Environmental Ethics: Philosophical and Policy Perspectives*. Burnaby, B.C.: Simon Fraser University, 1986.

_____. "Nature for the Sake of Nature." In Monte Hummel, ed., *Endangered Spaces*. Toronto: Key Porter Books, 1989.

_____. "Les implications écologiques du caractère impératif de l'immortalité de l'homme." *Frontières* 5/2 (Automne 1992).

Livingston, John R. "The World Conservation Strategy as a Dystopian Vision." *Undercurrents* 1 (Spring 1989).

Lopez, Barry Holstun. *Of Wolves and Men*. New York: Charles Scribner's Sons, 1978.

Lorenz, Konrad. *King Solomon's Ring*. London: Methuen, 1952.

_____. *On Aggression*. New York: Harcourt, Brace, and World, 1966.

Lovelock, J.E. *Gaia, A New Look at Life on Earth*. Oxford: Oxford University Press, 1979.

Magee, Bryan. *Popper*. Glasgow: Fontana/Collins, 1975.

Marcuse, Herbert. *One-Dimensional Man*. Boston: Beacon Press, 1964.

Martin, Paul S., and H.E. Wright, Jr., eds. *Pleistocene Extinctions: The Search for a Cause*. New Haven: Yale University Press, 1967.

Mech, L. David. *The Wolf*. Garden City, N.Y.: Natural History Press, 1970.

Meeker, Joseph W. *The Comedy of Survival*. New York: Charles Scribner's Sons, 1974.

Montagu, M.F. Ashley, ed. *Man and Aggression*. London: Oxford University Press, 1968.

Mowat, Farley. *Virunga: The Passion of Dian Fossey*. Toronto: Seal Books, 1988.

_____. *Rescue the Earth!: Conversations with the Green Crusaders*. Toronto: McClelland and Stewart, 1990.

Myers, Norman, ed. *GAIA: An Atlas of Planet Management*. Garden City, N.Y.: Anchor Press/Doubleday, 1984.

_____. *The Sinking Ark*. Oxford: Pergamon Press, 1979.

Naess, Arne. "The Shallow and the Deep, Long-Range Ecology Movement." *Inquiry* 16 (1973), 95–100.

Nomad Films International Pty. Ltd. *The Intruders*. South Melbourne, Australia, 1982.

Novak, Milan, James A. Baker, Martyn E. Obbard, and Bruce Malloch eds. *Wild Furbearer Management and Conservation in North America*. Ontario: Ministry of Natural Resources, 1987.

Odum, Eugene P. *Basic Ecology*. Philadelphia: Saunders College Publishing, 1983.

_____. *Ecology and Our Endangered Life-Support Systems*. Sunderland, Mass.: Sinauer Associates, 1989.

Ophuls, William. *Ecology and the Politics of Scarcity*. San Francisco: W.H. Freeman, 1977.

Osborn, Fairfield, Jr. *Our Plundered Planet*. Boston: Little, Brown, 1948.

Paddock, William, and Paul Paddock. *Famine — 1975!*. Boston: Little, Brown, 1967.

(H.R.H. The Prince) Philip, Duke of Edinburgh, and James Fisher. *Wildlife Crisis*. New York: Cowles Book Company, 1970.

Popper, Karl. *The Poverty of Historicism*. London: Routledge and Kegan Paul, 1961.

_____. *Objective Knowledge: An Evolutionary Approach*. Oxford: Oxford University Press, 1972.

Porksen, Uwe. Discussion of "plastic words," Canadian Broadcasting Corporation radio series *Ideas*, produced by David Cayley, 1993.

Regan, Tom. "The Case for Animal Rights" in Peter Singer, ed., *In Defense of Animals*. Oxford: Basil Blackwell, 1985.

Regier, Henry, and J. Bruce Falls, eds. *Exploding Humanity*. Toronto: Anansi, 1969.

Rollin, Bernard E. *Animal Rights and Human Morality*. Buffalo: Prometheus Books, 1981.

_____. *The Unheeded Cry*. Oxford: Oxford University Press, 1989.

Roots, Clive. *Animal Invaders*. Newton Abbot: David and Charles, 1976.

Routley, Richard, and Val Routley. "Human Chauvinism and Environmental Ethics." in D.S. Mannison, M.A. McRobbie, and R. Routley, eds., *Environmental Philosophy*. Department of Philosophy, Research School of Social Sciences, Australian National University, 1980.

Rowe, J. Stan. *Home Place: Essays on Ecology*. Edmonton: NeWest Publishers, 1990.

222

Rowell, Thelma. "The Concept of Dominance." *Behavioral Biology* 11 (1974), 131–54.

Russell, Dale A. *An Odyssey in Time: The Dinosaurs of North America.* Toronto: University of Toronto Press in association with the National Museum of Natural Sciences, 1989.

Sachs, Wolfgang. "The Archaeology of the Development Idea." *Interculture* 23/4 (Fall 1990).

Saint Exupéry, Antoine de. *The Little Prince.* New York: Harbrace Paperbound Library, 1971.

Sauer, Carl O. "The Agency of Man on Earth" in William L. Thomas Jr., ed., *Man's Role in Changing the Face of the Earth.* Chicago: University of Chicago Press, 1956.

Schjelderup-Ebbe, Thorlief. "Beitrage zur Sozialpsychologie des Haushuhns." *Zeitschrift zur Psychologie* 88 (1922), 225–52.

Scholtmeijer, Marian. *Animal Victims in Modern Fiction: From Sanctity to Sacrifice.* Toronto: University of Toronto Press, 1993.

Serpell, James. *In the Company of Animals: A Study of Human-Animal Relationships.* Oxford: Basil Blackwell, 1986.

Sessions, George. "Ecocentrism and the Greens: Deep Ecology and the Environmental Task." *The Trumpeter* 5/2 (Spring 1988).

Shepard, Paul. *The Tender Carnivore and the Sacred Game.* New York: Charles Scribner's Sons, 1973.

_____. *Nature and Madness.* San Francisco: Sierra Club Books, 1982.

Shepard, Paul, and Barry Sanders. *The Sacred Paw: The Bear in Nature, Myth, and Literature.* New York: Viking, 1985.

Shettleworth, Sara J. "Learning and Behavioural Ecology." In J.R. Krebs and N.B. Davies, eds., *Behavioural Ecology: An Evolutionary Approach.* Oxford: Blackwell Scientific Publications, 1984.

Singer, Peter. *Animal Liberation.* New York: Avon Books, 1975.

Singer, Peter, ed., *In Devense of Animals.* Oxford: Basil Blackwell, 1985.

Smuts, Barbara M., Dorothy L. Cheney, Robert M. Seyfarth, Richard W. Wrangham, and Thomas T. Struhsaker, eds., *Primate Societies.* Chicago: University of Chicago Press, 1987.

Stewart, Kelly J., and Alexander H. Harcourt. "Gorillas: Variation in Female Relationships" in Barbara B. Smuts et al., eds., *Primate Societies.* Chicago: University of Chicago Press, 1987.

Stone, Christopher. "Should Trees Have Standing? — Toward Legal Rights for Natural Objects." *Southern California Law Review* 45 (1972), 450.

Storr, Anthony. *Human Aggression*. Harmondsworth: Penguin, 1968.

_____. *Human Destructiveness*. New York: William Morrow, 1972.

Teilhard de Chardin, Pierre. *The Phenomenon of Man*. New York: Harper and Row, 1959.

_____. *Man's Place in Nature*. New York: Harper and Row, 1966.

Tennessen T., and R.J. Hudson. "Traits Relevant to the Domestication of Herbivores." *Applied Animal Ethology* 7 (1981), 87–102.

Thomas, William L., Jr., ed. *Man's Role in Changing the Face of the Earth*. Chicago: University of Chicago Press, 1956.

Toffler, Alvin. *The Third Wave*. New York: William Morrow, 1980.

Van Valen, Leigh. "Late Pleistocene Extinctions." *Proceedings of the North American Paleontological Convention*, 1969.

Vogt, William. *Road to Survival*. New York: William Sloane Associates, 1948.

Ward, Barbara, and Rene Dubos. *Only One Earth*. Harmondsworth: Penguin, 1972.

Welty, Joel Carl. *The Life of Birds*. New York: Alfred A. Knopf, 1963.

Wilson, Peter J. *The Domestication of the Human Species*. New Haven: Yale University Press, 1988.

The World Commission on Environment and Development. *Our Common Future*. Oxford: Oxford University Press, 1987.

Worster, Donald. *Nature's Economy: The Roots of Ecology*. Garden City, N.Y.: Anchor Books/Doubleday, 1979.

INDEX